W9-AOB-964

A SENSE OF DUTY

Jewish Sources Speak Books
Eugene B. Borowitz, Editor

A SENSE OF DUTY, Simcha Kling
WHAT IS MAN?, Arnold J. Wolf

A SENSE OF DUTY

Rabbi Simcha Kling

A B'NAI B'RITH BOOK

The B'nai B'rith Department of Adult Jewish Education has as its purpose to stimulate and promote the study of Judaism among adult Jews. Through annual Institutes of Judaism, year-round discussion groups, and authoritative and readable publications, it helps individuals and groups plan study programs on the religious-cultural heritage of the Jewish-people.

In memory of
Benjamin Leeman

Library of Congress Catalogue Card Number 68–31849
Manufactured in the United States of America

FOREWORD

Each volume of *The Jewish Sources Speak* books is designed to give the modern reader insight into a major theme of Judaism as expressed in its classic texts, particularly the post-Biblical. The readings have been selected with two basic criteria in mind: their relevance to the general concept around which each book centers and their representativeness of their Jewish literary genre. Only selections which treat at some length of the specific idea involved are utilized so as to afford the reader an in-depth exposure to each particular style of Jewish expression.

In the interests of clarity and readability, a few liberties have been permitted in the rendering of the passages. In certain instances, for example, repetitious material has been deleted. Almost all the texts are freely paraphrased rather than translated literally. Countering the loss in specific literary styles is, hopefully, a gain in the more central goal of communicating direct understanding of the ideas and thought processes involved. The texts are printed almost entirely without notes or the kind of commentary which usually accompanies them to clarify their intent. Instead, the commentary is incorporated into the texts themselves.

To further facilitate understanding of the way in which the various literary forms and intellectual patterns have contributed to an integrated Jewish life style, the selections are not arranged chronologically in order of composition but appear in terms of their thematic concerns. Where existing translations have been reprinted appropriate acknowledgments are made. Otherwise renderings are by the author of the specific volume.

This approach to Jewish ideas via the classic texts of Judaism makes it possible to present only the most significant aspects of each concept. There is intentionally no concluding or summary chapter. It is hoped that the thoughtful reader, introduced in this way to some of the Jewish classics, will be encouraged to go on to available translations of the full works. Thus familiarized with an important and relevant area of Jewish belief and of the varied Jewish literature in which it has been expressed and developed, he will be better equipped to tackle the Jewish sources themselves.

For critical reading of the manuscript and for numerous helpful suggestions, I am indebted to Dr. Ira Eisenstein, Dr. Louis L. Kaplan and Rabbi Norman Lamm. For general editing and for preparing the manuscript for press, my thanks go to Mrs. Lily Edelman, Director of B'nai B'rith's Commission on Adult Jewish Education; and for seeing the book through the press, to Miss Naomi Thompson, the Commission's Director of Production and Promotion.

Finally, a warm word of appreciation goes to Professor Oscar I. Janowsky, former Chairman of the Publications Committee of the Commission, under whose leadership this project was originally conceived and approved.

Eugene B. Borowitz,
General Editor

Contents

INTRODUCTION

The Torah proclaims the goal of Judaism: to sanctify life and invest it with holiness. The aim of Torah is to transform an ordinary folk, the Jewish people, into "a kingdom of priests and a holy nation." It does not seek to accomplish this by magical formula or logical argument. As far back as Biblical times, the prime emphasis of Judaism has been on conduct, its religious concern has been action. The people of Israel has been taught what to do: how to maintain a religious sensitivity, how to fashion a just society, how to meet the changes of season and history without wavering. All this and more were spelled out in detail.

The position of Judaism can be understood more clearly if contrasted with its daughter religion, Christianity. The Christian tradition stresses the imperative: "Believe!" Its major emphasis is on faith as the means to salvation. On the other hand, the Jewish tradition commands: "Observe!" It insists that deed is the key to religious fulfillment. This is not to say that Christianity ignores the problem of how men should live or that Judaism pays no heed to matters of faith. Each is concerned with both belief and practice: the Christian faith implies a Christian way of life; the Jewish way of life implies a Jewish faith.

Nevertheless, a sharp difference does exist. While Christianity preaches: "Believe and you shall be saved!," Judaism insists that what matters most is the way men live. Since its goal is the creation of a godly society, it does not focus on man's innermost motivations. Indeed, it welcomes the proper action even if performed for the wrong reason: the very doing of a virtuous act can acquaint the doer with awareness of the good. The Rabbis of the Mishnah put it this way: through performing an act *not* for its own sake one may end up doing it for its own sake. Judaism emphasizes the act first and the intent second, though a unity of both is preferable. The validity of this principle is frequently borne out: those who profess love sometimes perpetuate the most hateful deeds, and those who preach mercy become utterly deaf to the cries of the unfortunate. On the other hand, many a simple man has, in the face of danger, fed the hungry, clothed the naked, saved the desolate.

Thus, the traditional position of Judaism is that belief must be reflected in a way of life, that faith has to be translated into deeds to be valid. It prefers discipline to principles, habit to speculation. It is devoted to changing lives, transforming a people, redeeming real history. That is why it concentrates so much on Jewish duty.

In this context the terms *mitzvot* (commandments) and *halakhah* (law) are both intimately involved in the concept of Jewish duty; indeed, they are its most obvious structure. But neither is broad enough to encompass all that Jewish tradition expects of the Jew. Many virtues have been inculcated through the extensive realm of lore (*aggadah*) and teaching. Others have become a natural part of the folk inheritance, transmitted by parents to children and no less effective for not being formalized or institutionalized.

For this reason Torah, the term which comes closest to defining the essence of Judaism, cannot be rendered as "law." It is better understood as "instruction," with overtones of divine obligation. Nor can Jewish duty be dismissed as legalism, as some polemic teachers have done.

Jewish duty necessarily encompasses all of life. Family and charity, hygiene and social welfare, business relations and socializing, liturgy and government—all come under its purview. Duties toward God lead to duties toward self, toward the Jewish people, toward society as a whole, and back again. Judaism is not simply a religion, a church. The Jewish way of life is more than "religious"; its involvement with everyday life is basic.

As a result, Judaism imposes few limitations in the realm of abstract thought. Individuals are free to think largely as they wish and to discuss their views without restriction of dogma. Jewish duties provide the structure of existence; thus Judaism is elastic enough to include within its scope various theological and philosophical tendencies. What is important is not one specific Jewish concept of God but the fact that the individual lives a life of service to Him. Any concept of God which makes such a life possible is acceptable. Whether one does *tz'dakah* (gives charity) because the law requires it or because he can formulate a theology of philanthropy is less important than that the help is forthcoming.

Judaism thus gives special recognition to the differences that exist in men's temperaments. Some are bright, others dull; some are sophisticated, others naive; some are pure-hearted, others devious. All are superior to the beast and have the potential to raise themselves to high humanity. All are children of God and are expected to serve Him with their talents, in their way.

The way to achieve this is not left to individual caprice or haphazard experimentation. A system of duties has been developed which every Jew is taught and which every Jewish community encourages. Their fulfillment results in the full flowering of the man and the Jew, of the Jewish man. The pagan, who sees all of existence solely in terms of the physical and the sensual, may care only for the gratification of immediate desires and needs. The Jew has been oriented differently. His duties do not negate the physical aspects of life but insist that they be sanctified. Wine, money, sex, all find their proper place in the Jewish way of life. Jewish duty has never required a monastery or the hermit's life; its concern is with men in this world, participating in normal human society. Its specifics vary, adjusting partially to time and place, but the basic duties of the Jewish response to God and the world remain constant.

These standards have not been set beyond normal reach. Just as man is regarded as being more than a beast, so is he recognized as a human rather than an ethereal being. The responsibilities imposed upon him are not utopian but in keeping with that classic delineation in the Book of Deuteronomy:

> Surely this Instruction which I enjoin upon
> you this day is not too baffling for you
> nor is it beyond reach. It is not in

> heaven, that you should say: "Who among
> us can go up to the heavens and get it for
> us, and impart it to us, that we may
> observe it?" Neither is it beyond the
> sea, that you should say: "Who among us
> can pass to the other side of the sea
> and get it for us and impart it to us,
> that we may observe it?" No, the thing
> is very close to you, in your mouth, and
> in your heart, that you may observe it.
> (30:11–14)

What was enjoined then and later by the sages over the centuries is both possible and attainable. The duties which the Jew is bidden to fulfill are to enable him to develop to the utmost his physical, mental and spiritual dimensions. Their neglect can result in his being less than a complete person; and it can impede the creation of that just society for which all men wait and without which no individual can claim to have found his personal fulfillment.

To delineate the duties of a Jew is no simple matter. Just as all aspects of life are interrelated and constitute an organic whole, so too with the Jewish life style. Each area of activity is connected to other areas. Ethics and ritual, nationalism and internationalism, the individual and society, man and God—all are so interwoven and intertwined that any attempt to explore one leads, almost imperceptibly, to an exploration of the others. Yet, if we are to comprehend the whole, we must isolate the components and look at them separately.

I

BEING A DECENT PERSON

Since Judaism is a religion of duty and much more than that, a book on Jewish duty will be most faithful to its spirit by beginning with a discussion of the importance of transcending one's obligations. For Jewish law exists to create persons of character who in turn will form a holy community. That cannot be achieved by rule and training alone. It must be equally a matter of inner striving and accomplishment.

Thus, *halakhah,* the legal system that directs and guides the Jewish community, recognizes that there are ethical and moral responsibilities that cannot be made a part of the law yet are crucial to Judaism's high aspirations. For example, hospitality is deemed a virtue, but whether one is merely courteous or genuinely gracious as a host depends on personal character. Honesty in business is expected, but the law cannot dictate such scrupulous behavior that the individual will always be beyond suspicion.

The single prescription of the entire Mishnah chosen by the Rabbis for inclusion in the Jewish daily service (so that all Jews would at least do some study) begins as follows: "These are the things that cannot be measured," it states. It then proceeds to enumerate various categories of charity as well as the study of Torah. "These are the things which a person benefits from in this world, yet reaps their full reward in the world-to-come: honoring father and mother, deeds of lovingkindness, eagerness in attending the study-house, welcoming guests, visiting the sick, marrying off a bride, attending the dead, devotion in prayer, and making peace between a man and his fellow."

The Rabbis had a term for doing more than the minimum required of one. They spoke of acting "within the bounds of law." This has the sense of not exercising one's full legal advantages but is better understood in the modern sense of going "beyond the call of duty." The truly ethical personalities not only did what they were supposed to do but voluntarily did more. Their lives reflected not only discipline but, through it and beyond it, love and mercy, goodness and humility. Such qualities cannot be specifically defined or quantitatively measured, but they are the hallmark of a good human being, the indispensable characteristic of a man who reflects his having been created in God's image.

A unique emphasis of Jewish piety has been its insistence that man is called on to develop his mind as well as his soul since both are gifts of God. God is to be served by the intellect as well as by the emotions. Faith and reason are partners, not antagonists. Through the centuries, therefore, the Rabbis objected strongly to blind faith, superstition and magic. Though they insisted that God "cures the sick" yet they made it a duty to use the physician's art, refusing to rely on faith healing.

Even Jewish mysticism is distinguished by its intellectualism and intense speculative quality, and involves regular study of the sacred texts to develop the mystic's mental faculties. The famous Habad Hasidic master, Rabbi Schneour Zalman of Ladi, once remarked: "Virtue arising from reason is higher than virtue which is not founded on reason."

Yet, on balance, there is recognition of the limitations of man's reasoning powers. Logic does not necessarily engender lovingkindness, concern and consideration. Man's humanity to man stems from something deeper, his faith in God as the motive and criterion for his behavior. Reason, man's greatest ally in achieving that goal, cannot be slighted. Yet beyond thinking lie being and living. Judaism never loses sight of the whole man and by rule and, what is more than rule, tries to bring him into full or holy being.

1

Developing Character

Judaism demands that the Jew be a person of good character. Its expectations are expressed in a Talmudic legend which states that the first question put to one who arrives before the Throne of Judgment is neither: "Did you study the law?" nor "Did you trust in the coming of the Messiah?" The question is: "Were you honorable and faithful in your dealings with your fellow man?" Without decent upright people, the whole Jewish tradition would fail of its purpose. The ordinary Jew has never been a religious superman, but he has the possibility, if he follows the teachings of his faith and the style of his community, to become a moral, compassionate person. Judaism has created such individuals throughout its history.

This concern for human decency finds expression throughout Jewish literature. Particularly interesting are the wills written by fathers to impress their children with the importance of living ethically. The origins of this genre, called Ethical Wills, are obscure. Many of the Biblical heroes gave moral advice together with their final blessings to their children. A similar practice is recorded as typical of many of the Rabbis in Talmudic literature. In the apocryphal literature, a father's dying became the literary device for important teaching, as in *The Testament of the Twelve Patriarchs*.

Yet it is only much later, after 1000 C.E., that we begin to discover written Ethical Wills in the Jewish community. Some scholars have sought the impetus for this development in the Hebrew word for "will," which is analogous to that for "commandment." Judaism had taught the father that his major bequest to his children was his teaching rather than his goods. Jews who took their Judaism seriously gave it this literary expression and did so in increasing numbers through the nineteenth century. Some of these wills, either because their authors were great men or their content was of intrinsic interest, circulated widely in manuscript and were later reprinted. There is good reason to believe that many were written as much for the larger Jewish community as for the specific families.

The will which follows is that of Rabbi Asher ben Yehiel, who was born in Germany in 1250 and died in Spain in 1327. Rabbi Asher, better known as the "Rosh," was an eminent Talmudic scholar whose compendium of rabbinic laws was later printed in most editions of the Talmud as basic to the discussions of subsequent scholars. The Rosh's ethical treatise has been termed "The Rule" or "The Rule for the Health of the Soul (*Piskei ha-Rosh*)."

Rabbi Asher's rule clearly reflects Jewish values of pre-modern times. As moral standards of the past are increasingly challenged in our day, many persons are quite confused about the meaning of goodness. Yet Rabbi Asher's testament of six centuries ago seems both contemporary and relevant in its insights and understandings regarding human character.

FROM

The Rule of the Rosh

These are the things about which you must be careful if you want to elude the snares of death and to bask in the true light of life.

Do not be quick to quarrel, rather be careful not to deceive your fellow-man either in matters of money or of speech, nor to let your motives toward him come from envy or hate. Keep far from oaths and rash vows, from frivolity and anger, for these confuse both the spirit and the mind. Do not take the name of God in vain nor use it in improper places.

Rely not on frail human beings nor place your hope in gold; if you do, you have taken the first step toward idolatry. Instead, distribute your money freely; God will make good any deficit. Regard your virtues lightly and your vices seriously.

Magnify the mercies of Him who made you and who provides for your sustenance at all times. Do not do the right thing because you expect a reward nor avoid the wrong thing because you fear punishment; do what you do out of a sense of the love of God.

Regard the expenditure of your money as less important than the expenditure of your words; issue no base coin from your lips and weigh carefully what you say. Keep what you hear to yourself even if you are not pledged to confidence. If you hear a report from someone, do not say: "I have heard it already!"

Get accustomed to wake at dawn and to get out of bed at the song of the birds. Do not be lazy but rather rise as one eager to serve his Maker. Do not be a drunkard or a glutton lest you forget your Creator and fall into sin. Do not look with admiration at one who is richer than you but do pay attention to one who has less than you.

However, when it comes to serving God and being in awe of Him, then imitate the one who is greater than you rather than your inferior. Rejoice when you hear reproof; accept instruction and advice. Do not lord it over your fellow-men but be humble of spirit. Do not speak with insolence nor be haughty, for whoever does this rejects the fear of heaven. Never do in private what you would be ashamed to do in public, saying: "Who will see me?"

Do not raise your hand against your neighbor. Circulate no false reports and slander no man. If people talk to you in an unseemly manner, do not be quick to retort insolently. Let no man hear you in the street: do not bellow like a beast; let your voice be soft. Never embarrass anyone publicly. The first precaution against doing wrong to another is to avoid wanting what he has.

Never be weary of making friends; consider a single enemy as one too many. If you have a faithful friend, hold fast to him; he is a precious possession and you should treasure him. But do not encourage friendship by hypocrisy and adulation; do not be two-faced.

Do not remain angry with your fellow-man for a single day but humble yourself and ask forgiveness. Do not be proud, saying: "I am the injured party; let him make the first overtures." Rather, before you retire every night, forgive anyone who has offended you. If people revile you or curse you, do not answer; be of the insulted and not of the insulters.

Be steady in following the middle road in satisfying your appetites. Neither be accessible to all nor a recluse from all. In all matters of morality, stick to the middle of the road. Do not indulge in many celebrations; remember that life is short, that you come from dust and that you are destined to be with worms. Do not be offended at trifles lest you accumulate enemies without cause. Pry not into other people's secrets. Be not overbearing toward the people of your community; yield to the wishes of others.

Make God's will your own. Rejoice in your portion whether it be great or small. Pray continually to God that He help you follow His laws. Never show ingratitude, but respect every person who helps you earn the necessities of life. Never utter a falsehood, but be loyal to all men, irrespective of creed. Be not slow to offer greetings to everyone, Jew or Gentile, and never give a fellow-man cause for resentment.

Always be hospitable to wayfarers; welcome them cheerfully. When they go on their way, provide them with food for their journey, accompany them part of the way, and let them leave with a cheerful farewell.

Do not harm your body by imbibing; you may betray yourself into ugly acts or coarse speech and afterward be remorseful. Never be angry with your wife; if you put her off with one hand, draw her near with the other.

Be responsive to the call of charity at all times. Never give less than a half-shekel annually and at one time. Give every month and every week as much as you can spare. Do not let any day pass without making some small contribution before prayer. When your means reach a titheable amount, set aside a tithe.

Enjoy not food or drink without a blessing before and after, rendering thanks to Him who has satisfied your longing soul.

Cover your head when you mention God's Name. Let your innermost being be stirred when you speak of Him. Do not be among those of whom Scriptures say: *With their mouths and with their lips they honor Me, but they have removed their hearts far from Me.* Wash your hands before praying and before eating.

Sanctify yourself in all things: never behave with levity; let the fear of God always be upon you. Before meals and before going to bed, read the Torah regularly and derive from its pages topics to talk about at the table. In all matters needing direction, direct your household in accordance with the Torah.

Do not pray mechanically, for prayer is the service of the heart. Do you not become angry if your child talks to you insincerely? How then should you, an insignificant nothing, act in the presence of the King of the universe? Do not be like a servant who spoils something precious that has been entrusted to him for his own good. Such a one could not stand before the King!

Do not neglect to confess your sins morning and evening nor to remember Zion and Jerusalem with a broken heart and bitter tears. When you recite the verse which bids you love the Lord your God, speak as one ready to sacrifice life and substance for Him, thus fulfilling the words of the Psalmist: *For Your sake are we killed every day.* Yet have a wholehearted confidence in Him and believe in His providence. Day and night, let your lips make mention of Him. When you lie down, luxuriate in His love and you will find it in your dreams. When you awake, you will delight in Him and He will direct your paths. So fulfill all your virtuous acts in the spirit of walking humbly before Him. This is the service which He has chosen: this is the service acceptable in His sight.

2

Going Beyond the Law

The full goal of Jewish tradition is reflected by the two categories into which rabbinic thought is divided. *Halakhah* represents the discipline necessary in life; *halakhic* or legal literature is concerned with establishing the laws that regulate Jewish behavior. The second realm, *aggadah,* represents the non-legal, the history and folklore, the business and personal norms, the poetry, prayers and mystic flights, the tales of great and simple men. *Halakhah* details the practices that structure religious living; *aggadah* speaks of beliefs and ideals.

Certain sages were masters of *halakhah,* others of *aggadah.* None, however, chose one to the exclusion of the other. *Halakhah* alone would be too confining, *aggadah* alone too anarchic. *Halakhah* and *aggadah* were integrated into a totality that spell out a rounded religious way of life. Man must be more than a creature of law or of poetry to be worthy before God.

The tale which follows illustrates the duty of the Jew to obey the law yet to go beyond it. It reflects the basic teachings of Hasidism, which began in the eighteenth century as a rebellion against the dry intellectualism of the traditional schools here represented by what someone has called the "dour" rationalist of Eastern Europe, the Lithuanian or Litvak. Hasidism stresses the joyful, enthusiastic love of God who is to be seen in all men and in all of nature. It brought a renewed personal and subjective emphasis to a Judaism which had become overly preoccupied with law and study. It brought the humble people a great sense of personal involvement for it also taught that the Hasidic leader, the *rebbe,* was particularly close to God and could intervene in heaven on behalf of his followers.

Hasidism took hold particularly in the central and southern

part of East Europe. It did not gain a stronghold in Lithuania where the older East European intellectual tradition was maintained in full force. The Hasidim accordingly regarded the Lithuanians or Litvaks as excessively bookish, clever for the sake of cleverness, skeptics who refused to grant the wonders performed by the Hasidic *rebbes.* In this story, the cynical Litvak finally learns the truth of the saying of the Hasidic master, Rabbi Levi Yitzhak of Berditchev: "Whether a man really loves God can be determined by the love he bears toward his fellow-man."

If Not Higher is a story written by Yehudah Leib Peretz (1852–1915), who, with Sholom Aleichem and Mendele Mocher Sforim, helped to create modern Yiddish literature. Peretz was a thoroughly emancipated, secular Jew who had graduated from the university as a lawyer but eventually came to work for the Jewish community of Warsaw. He was attracted to Hasidic types in his short stories for they allowed him to express the pain and longing, the suffering and hopes of the common Jew. There was a note of irony in much that he wrote. While he does not hesitate to criticize the Jewish people, his writings are suffused with a love of Jewish ideals and concerns. In the period before World War I, Peretz' many poems, essays and plays, as well as his short stories, were among the major cultural achievements of East European Jewry.

In the story that follows, the Rabbi of Nemirov exemplifies the teaching of the prophets that ritual observances have meaning only if they lead to justice and righteousness. Hasidism as a whole may be said to be an elaboration of Rabbi Meir's dictum: "Let your works exceed your learning."

If Not Higher

BY Y. L. PERETZ

Early every Friday morning, at the time of the *selihot* prayers,* the Rabbi of Nemirov would disappear, vanish! He was nowhere to be seen—neither in the synagogue nor in the two Houses of Study nor at a *minyan*. And he was certainly not at home. His door stood open; whoever wished, could go in and out; no one would steal from the rabbi. But not a living creature was within. Where could the rabbi be?

Where should he be? In heaven, no doubt. A rabbi has plenty of business to take care of just before the Days of Awe. Jews, God bless them, have many needs: a livelihood, peace, health, and proper mates. They want to be pious and good, but our sins are so great, and Satan of the thousand eyes watches the whole earth from one end to the other. What he sees he reports; he denounces, informs. Who can help us if not the rabbi!

That's what the people thought.

But once a Litvak came, and he laughed. You know those Lithuanians. They think little of the Holy Books but stuff themselves with Talmud and law. So this Litvak points to a passage in the Gemara—it sticks in your eyes—where it is written that even Moses, our Teacher, did not ascend to heaven during his lifetime but remained suspended two and a half feet below. Go argue with a Litvak!

So where can the rabbi be?

"That's not my business," said the Litvak, shrugging. Yet all the while—what a Litvak can do!—he is scheming to find out.

That same night, right after the evening prayers, the Litvak

* During the days preceding Rosh Hashanah, it is customary to recite special penitential prayers, *selihot,* each morning. Since the Day of Judgment is approaching, it is a time of awe and reverence.

steals into the rabbi's room, slides under the rabbi's bed, and waits. He'll watch all night and discover where the rabbi vanishes and what he does during the *selihot* services.

Someone else might have got drowsy and fallen asleep, but a Litvak is never at a loss; he recited a whole tractate of the Talmud by heart!

Just before dawn, he hears the call to prayers.

The rabbi has already been awake for a long time. The Litvak has heard his groaning for a whole hour. Whoever has heard the Rabbi of Nemirov groan knows how much sorrow for all Israel, how much suffering, lies in each groan. A man's heart might break, hearing it. But a Litvak is made of iron; he listens and remains where he is. The rabbi, long life to him, lies on his bed, and the Litvak under the bed.

Then the Litvak hears the beds in the house begin to creak; he hears people jumping out of their beds, mumbling a few Jewish words, pouring water on their fingernails, banging doors. Everyone has left. It is again quiet and dark; a bit of light from the moon shines through the shutters.

(Afterward the Litvak admitted that when he found himself alone with the rabbi, a great fear took hold of him. Goose pimples spread across his skin, and the roots of his earlocks pricked him like needles. A trifle: to be alone with the rabbi at the time of *selihot!* But a Litvak is stubborn. So he quivered like a fish in water and remained where he was.)

Finally, the rabbi, long life to him, arises. First he does what befits a Jew. Then he goes to the clothes closet and takes out a bundle of peasant clothes: linen trousers, high boots, a coat, a big felt hat, and a long wide leather belt studded with brass nails. The rabbi gets dressed. From his coat pocket dangles the end of a heavy peasant rope.

The rabbi goes out. The Litvak follows him.

On the way the rabbi stops in the kitchen, bends down, takes an ax from under the bed, puts it in his belt, and leaves the house. The Litvak trembles but continues to follow.

The hushed dread of the Days of Awe hangs over the dark streets. Every once in a while a cry arises from some *minyan* reciting the *selihot* prayers, or from a sickbed. The rabbi hugs the sides of the streets, keeping to the shadow of the houses. He glides from house to house, and the Litvak after him. The Litvak hears the sound of his heartbeats mingling with the sound of the rabbi's heavy steps. But he keeps on going and follows the rabbi to the outskirts of the town.

A small wood stands behind the town.

The rabbi, long life to him, enters the wood. He takes thirty or forty steps and stops by a small tree. The Litvak, overcome by amazement, watches the rabbi take the ax out of his belt and strike the tree. He hears the tree creak and fall. The rabbi chops the tree into logs and the logs into sticks. Then he makes a bundle of the wood and ties it with the rope in his pocket. He puts the bundle of wood on his back, shoves the ax back into his belt, and returns to the town.

He stops at a back street beside a small broken-down shack and knocks at the window.

"Who is there?" asks a frightened voice. The Litvak recognizes it as the voice of a sick Jewish woman.

"I," answers the rabbi in the accent of a peasant.

"Who is I?"

Again the rabbi answers in Russian. "Vassil."

"Who is Vassil, and what do you want?"

"I have wood to sell, very cheap." And, not waiting for the woman's reply, he goes into the house.

The Litvak steals in after him. In the gray light of early morning he sees a poor room with broken, miserable furnishings. A sick woman, wrapped in rags, lies on the bed. She complains bitterly: "Buy? How can I buy? Where will a poor widow get money?"

"I'll lend it to you," answers the supposed Vassil. "It's only six groschen."

"And how will I ever pay you back?" said the poor woman, groaning.

"Foolish one," says the rabbi reproachfully. "See, you are a poor sick Jew, and I am ready to trust you with a little wood. I am sure you'll pay. While you, you have such a great and mighty God and you don't trust him for six cents."

"And who will kindle the fire?" said the widow. "Have I strength to get up? My son is at work."

"I'll kindle the fire," answers the rabbi.

As the rabbi put the wood into the oven he recited, in a groan, the first portion of the *selihot*. As he kindled the fire and the wood burned brightly, he recited, a bit more joyously, the second part of the penitential prayers. When the fire was set he recited the third portion, and then he shut the stove.

The Litvak who saw all this remained in town and became a disciple of the rabbi.

And ever after, when another disciple told how the Rabbi of Nemirov used to ascend to heaven at the time of *selihot,* the Litvak did not laugh. He only added quietly: "If not higher."

3

Using Reason

Judaism does not exalt rationalism but neither does it spurn man's capacity to think. Thus the Biblical heroes are not philosophers but prophets, and rabbinic tradition knows more of mysticism than of metaphysics. Both Bible and Talmud are concerned with man's potential to live nobly. Though this has remained the major focus of Jewish intellectuality, man's speculative probing has had a valued place in Judaism. The first of the petitions of the Jewish daily service is a plea for knowledge, an explicit philosophical tradition which became strong among Jews in the Middle Ages. In this literature, the highest valuation is placed on the role of reason in Jewish religious life.

Outstanding among the Jewish rationalists of the Middle Ages was Moses Maimonides, known by the initials of his Hebrew name as Rambam (1135–1204). He was born in Cordova, Spain, where he spent his youth in intensive study under the tutelage of his father, a noted scholar. When Jewish life became extremely hazardous, the Maimon family left Spain, spent a few years in North Africa, visited the Holy Land, and finally settled in Cairo. There, Maimonides became one of the outstanding physicians of the country, serving the Sultan as physician of the royal harem. He was simultaneously the spiritual leader of the Jewish community of Egypt and was regarded as the foremost religious authority of the Jewish world. A brilliant jurist, he was the first scholar to codify the vast body of Jewish law that had accumulated in the nearly one thousand years since the compilation of the Mishnah.

At the same time, Maimonides was fully at home in the Greek-Arab intellectual world of his age, a world of Aristotelian science and philosophy. He recognized that many Jews were uncertain of their faith because of the seemingly irrational character of some Jewish teachings. Maimonides' attempt to reconcile Judaism and the new science resulted in *Moreh Nevukhim* (*Guide for the Perplexed*), a classic of medieval Jewish philosophy.

Moreh Nevukhim is a fervent expression of its author's faith in reason. While Maimonides recognized the limitations of man's rational faculties and pointed out that there was a significant realm beyond reason, he asserted that man's capacity to think was his most important link to God. He dared to rank reason as the highest expression of the divine in human nature. Thus, *Moreh Nevukhim,* expressing faith in reason, is the classic formulation of the Jew's duty to use his intellect. Though not fully accepted by his own contemporaries, and indeed violently opposed by some, Maimonides has since been studied and discussed by Jews in every generation.

FROM

The Guide for the Perplexed

(*Part III, Chapter 51*)

BY MOSES MAIMONIDES

I will begin this chapter with a simile. A king is in his palace, and all his subjects are partly in the city and partly away. Of the former, some have their backs turned toward the king's palace and their faces in another direction. Some seek to reach the palace, turn toward it seeking to enter it and stand before him, but have not yet even seen its wall.

Of those that are eager to go to the palace, some reach it and go round about in search of the entrance gate; others have succeeded in entering into the inner court of the palace, thus getting to the place where the king lives. But even these subjects do not immediately see the king or speak to him. For, after having entered the inner part of the palace, another effort is required of them before they can stand before the king, see him at a distance or close by, and hear his words or speak to him.

I will now explain this simile. The people who are away are those who have no religious belief, neither one based on speculation nor one received by tradition. Such are the furthermost Turks that wander about in the north, the Kushites who live in the south, and those in our country who are like them. I consider them irrational beings and not truly human beings; they are below mankind but above the monkeys, since they have the form and shape of man and a mental faculty above that of the monkey.

Those who are in the city but have their backs turned toward the king's palace are those who possess religion, belief and thought, but follow false doctrines which they have either adopted in consequence of great mistakes made in their own speculations or received from others who misled them. Because of these doctrines, the more they seem to proceed, the more they recede from the royal palace. They are worse than the first class, and under certain circumstances it may become necessary to slay them and extirpate their doctrines in order that others should not be misled.

Those who desire to arrive at the palace and seek to enter it but have never yet seen it are the mass of religious people; the multitude that observe the divine commandments but are ignorant.

Those who arrive at the palace but go round about it are those who devote themselves exclusively to the study of the practical law; they believe in the traditional true principles of faith and learn the practical worship of God but are not trained in philosophical analysis of the principles of the law and do not endeavor to establish the truth of their faith by proof.

Those who undertake to investigate the principles of religion have come into the antechambers; and there is no doubt that these can also be divided into different grades. He who has succeeded in finding a proof for everything that can be proved, who has a true knowledge of God, so far as a true knowledge can be attained, and is near the truth, wherever an approach to truth is possible, has reached the palace in which the king lives.

My son, so long as you are engaged in studying the mathematical sciences and logic, you belong to those who go round about the palace in search of the gate . . . When you understand physics, you have entered the antechamber; and when, after completing the study of natural philosophy, you master metaphysics, you have entered the innermost court and are with the king in his dwelling. You have attained the degree of the wise men who themselves are men of different grades of perfection.

There are some who, having attained perfection in metaphysics, devote themselves entirely to God, exclude from their thought every other thing, and employ all their intellectual faculties in the study of the universe, in order to derive therefrom proof of the existence of God and to learn in whatever way possible how God rules all things. They form the class of those who have entered the king's council, namely the class of prophets.

One of these has attained so much knowledge and has concentrated his thoughts to such an extent on the idea of God that it could be said of him: *And he was with the Lord forty days;* during that holy communion he could ask questions of Him, receive answers, speak to Him and be addressed by Him, enjoying beatitude in that which he had obtained to such a degree that *he did neither eat bread nor drink water.* His intellectual energy was so predominant that all coarser functions of the body, especially those connected with the sense of touch, were in abeyance. Some prophets are only able to see, and of these some approach near and see, while others see from a distance . . .

We exhort those who have attained a knowledge of God to concentrate all their thoughts on God. This is the worship peculiar to those who have acquired a knowledge of the highest truths; and the more they reflect on Him and think of Him the more are they engaged in His worship.

Those, however, who think of God and frequently mention His name without any correct notion of Him, but merely follow some imagination or some theory received from another person are, in my opinion, like those who remain outside the palace and distant from it. In reality, they do not mention the name of God in truth nor do they reflect upon it. That which they imagine and mention does not correspond to any being in existence; it is a thing invented by their imagination . . . The true worship of God is only possible when correct notions of Him have previously been conceived.

When you have arrived by way of intellectual research at a knowledge of God and His works, then commence to devote yourselves to Him, try to approach Him and strengthen the intellect which is the link that joins you to Him. Thus Scripture says: *Unto you it was shown, that you might know that the Lord He is God. Know therefore this day and consider it in your heart that the Lord is God. Know you that the Lord is God.* Thus the law distinctly states that the highest kind of worship to which we refer in this chapter is only possible after the intellectual acquisition of the knowledge of God. For it is said: *To love the Lord your God, and to serve Him with all your heart and with all your soul.*

As we have shown several times, man's love of God is identical with His knowledge of Him. The divine service enjoined in these words must, accordingly, be preceded by the love of God. Our sages have pointed out to us that it is a service in the heart, which explanation I understand to mean this: man concentrates all his thoughts on the First Intellect and is absorbed in these thoughts as much as possible. David therefore commands his son, Solomon, these two things and exhorts him earnestly to do them: first, to acquire a true intellectual knowledge of God, and then to be earnest in His service after that knowledge has been acquired. For he says: *And you, Solomon my son, know you the God of your father and serve Him with a perfect heart . . . if you seek Him, He will be found by you; but if you forsake Him, He will cast you off forever.*

The exhortation refers to the intellectual conception, not to the imagination; for the latter are not called "knowledge" but *that which comes into your mind.* It has thus been shown that it must be man's aim, after having acquired the intellectual knowledge of God, to deliver himself up to Him and to have his heart continually filled with longing for Him. He accomplishes this generally by seclusion and retirement. Every pious man should therefore seek frequent isolation and should associate with others only in the case of necessity.

Note carefully: I have shown you that the intellect which emanates from God unto us is the link that joins us to God. You have it in your power to strengthen that bond if you choose to do so or to weaken it gradually till it breaks, if you prefer this. It will only become strong when you employ it in the love of God and seek that love in the way just explained; it will be weakened when you direct your thoughts to other things.

You must know that even if you were the wisest man in respect to the true knowledge of God, you break the bond between you and God whenever you entirely turn your thoughts to the food you need or any necessary business. You are then not with God and He is not with you. For that relation between you and Him is actually interrupted in those moments.

The pious were therefore particular to restrict the time in which they could not meditate upon the Name of God, and cautioned others about it, saying: "Let not your minds be vacant from reflections upon God." In the same sense did David say: *I have set the Lord before me always; because He is at my right hand, I shall not be moved;* i.e. I do not move my thoughts away from God; He is like my right hand which I do not forget even for a moment on account of the ease of its motions, and therefore I shall not be moved, I shall not fall.

Bear in mind that all such religious acts as reading the Torah, praying, and the performance of other commandments serve exclusively as the means of causing us to occupy and fill our mind with God's commandments, and free the mind from worldly business. We should act, as it were, as if we were in communication with God and undisturbed by any other thing.

If we, however, pray with the motion of our lips and our face toward the wall, but at the same time think of our business; if we read the Torah with our tongue while our heart is occupied with the building of our house and we do not think of what we are reading; if we perform the commandments only with our limbs, we are like those who are engaged in digging the ground or hewing wood in the forest and are not reflecting on the nature of these acts, by whom they are commanded or what is their object, you should not think you have accomplished anything . . .

I will now show you how to educate and train yourself in order to attain that great perfection.

The first thing you must do is this: turn your thoughts away from everything while you read the *shema* in all its paragraphs and do not content yourself with merely feeling devout when you read its first verse or first paragraph. When you have successfully practiced this for many years, try listening to the Torah when it is read in such a way that your heart and all your thoughts are occupied in reflecting upon what you read or hear. When you have mastered this, accustom yourself to having your mind free from all other thoughts when you read any portion of the other books of the prophets or when you say any blessing; aim to have your attention directed exclusively to the understanding of what you utter.

When you have succeeded in properly performing these acts of divine service and you have your thought, during their performance, entirely abstracted from worldly affairs, you may then occupy your mind with your wants and lesser desires, all sorts of worldly matters when you eat, drink, bathe, talk with your wife and little children, or when you converse with ordinary folk. These times, which are frequent and long, I think, will suffice for reflecting on everything that is necessary as regards business, household and health. But when you are engaged in the performance of religious duties, have your mind exclusively directed to what you are doing, as has been explained.

When, however, you are alone, when you are awake on your couch, be careful to meditate in such precious moments on nothing but the intellectual worship of God, that nearness to Him and that genuine being in His presence which I have described to you as contrasted to what is attained by the hollow emotions. I believe this high perfection can be attained by wise men by the above training.

II

CREATING A GOOD SOCIETY

How can one hope to be a religious person while living as part of an imperfect society? At various times in human history, there have been people who thought it religiously desirable to isolate themselves from the corrupting influences of communal life. One of the reasons for the great interest in the community of Essenes described in the Dead Sea Scrolls is that those Jews chose to live apart from the rest of the Jewish community. They went into the wilderness to join a religious order which imposed upon its members isolation, purity and strict discipline. They undoubtedly regarded the attainment of true piety as possible only in such segregated communities.

The Essenes were, however, a great Jewish exception. Rabbinic Judaism totally rejected such views, insisting that the Jew must live in and be part of society, no matter how imperfect that society might be. Hillel instructed the people: "Do not separate yourself from the community." The point is even more explicit in his saying: "In a place where there are no men, you try to be a man." These sentiments of both communal and individual responsibility for the welfare of society have been echoed and re-echoed by great Jewish teachers and sages down through the centuries.

Undoubtedly, living with others brings distractions and temptations. Yet, the road to holiness is not to be found by running away. Man cannot be fully man unless he associates with men and helps them to live a life of righteousness. That is why Judaism is concerned with creating a righteous community as well as noble individuals.

Even the medieval Jewish mystics—those who passionately sought to penetrate the "real" world that lies beyond the apparent one of the senses, and thus find intimate communion with God—did not divorce themselves from the Jewish community. They may have been more detached than others and, for brief spans, more isolated; but they married and became fathers of families, they observed *halakhah* and participated in synagogue life. In the mid-sixteenth century their piety suffused the whole town of Safed; in Hasidism the *rebbe's* community was all-important.

This social concern of Judaism is considered one of its most important and distinctive traits. The Bible includes legislation to protect the widow, the orphan and the poor, to save the man guilty of manslaughter, to preserve the dignity of the deaf and the blind and the aged. It has rules safeguarding the rights of both employer and employee, landowner and tenant. Its Messianic vision is of all nations living in peace and harmony.

In Talmudic times, soup kitchens were set up for the poor while communal agencies provided indigent brides with dowries, tended the ill and prepared the dead for burial. In the ghettos of later Europe, travelers were assured of safe lodging, students were provided with enough food to sustain themselves, and hospitals were established for the sick. When Jews left the Old World, they took with them their social teachings. To this day, Jewish communities in the Diaspora support hospitals, schools, family and vocational agencies, and a host of other social services.

From among the many social duties which Judaism propounds, we have chosen three. Responsibility toward the ill is typical of that concern for the unfortunate and powerless which is so much a part of the prophets' teachings about the will of God. The more positive and creative duties are represented by the obligation to educate the young. Both have as their goal the enhancement and preservation of life, which is the silver thread running through all other duties.

These duties, which are specially stressed in Judaism, are based upon the Jewish conception of God not as a logical abstraction or an intellectual construct but as the Holy One, blessed be He. As He is holy, so man must be holy; the

Rabbis understood this to mean that as God, in the Bible, is described as caring for men, so must men care for one another.

Jewish social concern stems directly from Jewish faith. It persists today largely as a legacy of the Jewish social heritage, even when religious faith itself has weakened.

4

Visiting the Sick

Judaism bids us accept illness and death as a part of life by imposing upon us an obligation to visit the sick and the bereaved. It is precisely when our fellow human beings feel deserted and forsaken that our presence can bring special healing.

For this reason Jewish tradition has long insisted that *bikkur holim,* visiting the sick, is a religious obligation, an act worthy of God Himself. While its observance cannot change society in and of itself, it symbolizes the concern of man for other men as the moral basis on which a good society must be built. According to legend, when Abraham was recuperating from his circumcision, God said to His angels: "Come, let us pay a visit to the sick." The angels refused, saying: "What is man that Thou art mindful of him? And the son of man that Thou visit him?" God, however, would not accept their retort, answering that He would go without them if need be, which He did, as we read in the story of Abraham's three visitors. If God performed such a deed, the Rabbis argued, man should do likewise.

The following passage on the duty to visit the sick comes from the Talmud, that encyclopedic record of the manifold and complex discussions carried on in the various schools of Palestine and Babylonia over a period of seven or eight hundred years. It is made up of two parts: the Mishnah, the code of Jewish law compiled from many traditions at the end of the second century; and the Gemara, compiled at the end of the fifth century, which contains the various discussions based upon the Mishnah. The Talmud contains legal discussions but much more. It touches upon every aspect of life: business and family, faith and folklore, medicine and science, ethics and popular practices. All of subsequent Judaism is rooted in the Talmud; its views and decisions shaped the course of Jewish life and thought.

Our selection is found in the tractate of *Nedarim* (39b–41b), which means "religious vows"; as often happens in the Talmud, the original discussion branches out, in this case to focus on visiting the sick. Typically too, many traditions, differing in time and origin and even in content, are then recorded. Most Talmudic discussions do not deal with a single issue at such length and generally have greater legal concern. Yet the depth of rabbinic feeling expressed here comes through with sufficient impact for us to see why *bikkur holim* became an accepted Jewish duty throughout the ages.

Clearly, visiting the sick was not a matter of etiquette but of divine command. Judaism insists that man's physical welfare is related to his spiritual well-being; physical health is therefore as important as spiritual health.

FROM

Talmud

(*Tractate Nedarim, 39b*)

There is a tradition: "There is no measure for visiting the sick." Rabbi Joseph said: "This means that the reward for visiting the sick is unlimited." Abaye retorted: "This cannot be the meaning because there is no definite measure of reward for any of the commandments. After all, we have been taught: 'Be just as careful about a seemingly minor precept as about an obviously important one, inasmuch as we do not know what rewards are given for which precepts.' " Abaye thus deduced that the phrase "no measure" referred to the manner of the performance of the precept, that is, that even a distinguished person should visit one less distinguished. Raba understood the phrase to refer to the number of visits and ruled that one should visit even a hundred times a day.

Rabbi Abba ben Rabbi Hanina said: "He who visits an invalid takes away a sixtieth of his pain." The Rabbis then said to him: "If that were true, let sixty people visit the ill person and he will be restored to health!"

Rabbi Abba replied: "It is a mathematical progression, like that taught in the School of Rabbi Judah Hanasi with regard to inheritances: each takes away a percentage of what is left. The first visitor takes away one-sixtieth of the illness; the second takes away one-sixtieth of the remaining illness, etc. Thus, visitors do not cure, but they certainly help." Rabbi Abba also specified that, for the visit to be effective, the visitor should be like the sick person—i.e. about the same age.

Once, it happened that Rabbi Helbo fell ill. Rabbi Kahana went to the scholars and told them, but no one paid him a visit. Rabbi Kahana thereupon rebuked the scholars by telling them the following story: one of Rabbi Akiba's disciples once fell ill and none of his colleagues called upon him. Rabbi Akiba, himself, thereupon visited the sick man. He found the room very neglected. He immediately gave orders to have it swept and cleaned. As a result, the disciple recovered. He said to Rabbi Akiba: "My master, you have revived me!" Rabbi Akiba thereupon taught: "Whoever does not visit the sick is like one who sheds blood."

When Rabbi Dimi was making one of his visits to Babylonia from the Land of Israel, he taught: "He who visits the sick causes him to live; he who does not causes him to die." How does the visitor do this? We might say that it is because he who visits prays that the sick man may live, while he who does not, so to speak, prays that he should die.

But can we really say that one who does not visit prays that the invalid should die? Let us put it this way: he who does not visit the sick does not pray that he should live or die. Hence, what Rabbi Dimi meant was that he who does not visit the sick does not pray, and by the lack of his prayers, which might have been accepted, he may be said to have caused the sick man's death.

Whenever Raba became ill, he would, on the first day, ask that it be kept secret lest the gossip affect his affairs. But after the first day, he instructed his servants to go and proclaim his illness in the market-place. His enemies, he hoped, would rejoice and thereby bring about the fulfillment of the verse: *Rejoice not when your enemy falls . . . lest the Lord see it and it displeases Him, and He turn away His wrath* (i.e. the cause of the illness) *from him.* He also hoped that his friends, upon learning of his illness, would pray for him.

Rab said: "He who visits the sick will be delivered from the punishments of hell, as it is written: *Blessed is he that considereth the poor* (Hebrew: *dal*); *the Lord will deliver him in the day of evil.* Rab argued that *dal* really means "the sick." It was used in this sense in describing the illness of King Hezekiah, and Absalom's pining away is called *dal.* Therefore, the first part of the original verse may be understood as: Blessed is he that considereth the sick. And the second part, with its reference to "the day of evil," refers to hell, as it is written: *The Lord hath made all things for Himself; yea, even the wicked for the day of evil,* which obviously means their punishment in hell.

What of the opposite? If one does visit, what is his reward? How can you ask: "What is his reward?" Has it not just been said that he will be delivered from the punishments of hell! But that reward refers to the life of the world-to-come. What is his reward in this world? It is given in the following verse: *The Lord will preserve him and keep him alive, and he shall be blessed upon the earth and Thou wilt not deliver him unto the will of his enemies.*

We may interpret this as follows: *The Lord will preserve him*—from the Evil Urge; *And keep him alive*—saving him from sufferings; *And he shall be blessed upon the earth*—that all will take pride in him; *And Thou wilt not deliver him unto the will of his enemies*—that he may gain friends like Naaman's, whose intercession caused him to be cured of his leprosy and not fair-weather friends like Rehoboam's, who were the cause of the division of the kingdom.

In connection with Rehoboam, let us note the teaching of

Rabbi Simeon ben Elazar who said: "If the young tell you to build and the old to destroy, hearken to the elders but not to the young, for the building of youth is destruction while the destruction of the old is building. In such matters, Rehoboam * is the classic example."

Rabbi Shisha ben Rabbi Idi said: "One should not visit the sick during the first three nor the last three hours of the day, since one might then forget to pray for the person. During the first three hours of the day, the illness is least serious. If you visit then, you might think him so well that you would neglect to pray for him. During the last three hours of the day, the illness is at its most virulent. If you visit then, you might assume that there was no help for the invalid, not even prayer."

Rabin said that Rab taught that we know the Almighty sustains the sick from the verse: *The Lord will strengthen him upon the bed of languishing*. He also said: We know from the same verse that the Divine Presence itself rests above an invalid's bed. The Hebrew word for "strengthen him" may be understood as "set Himself," thus making the verse mean: "The Lord doth set Himself upon the bed of languishing." Thus, the Divine Presence is there.

That is the reason it was taught: He who visits the sick will generally find him on a low bed. Therefore the visitor must not sit upon the bed or on a stool or a chair and thus sit above the patient. Rather let him come in dignified attire and sit below the level of the patient, for the Divine Presence rests above an invalid's bed . . .

Rabbi Alexandri said that Rabbi Hiyya bar Abba had taught: Only when a man's sins are forgiven him does he recover from his sickness. Thus, it is written: *Who forgiveth all thine iniquities, who healeth all thy diseases*. Rabbi Hamnuna said: He also returns to the days of his youth, for it is written: *His flesh shall be fresher than a child's; he shall return to the days of his youth.*

* Rehoboam, the son of Solomon, is held responsible for the split of the Jewish Kingdom of his father into two states, Israel and Judah. Neglecting the advice of his older counsellors to be gentle, he followed a policy of rigor as suggested by his youthful retainers. That precipitated the secession of the Northern Ten Tribes.

Rabbi Joseph interpreted the verse: *Thou hast turned his bed in his sickness* to mean that, in sickness, one can forget all one's learning. It happened once that Rabbi Joseph fell ill and he forgot what he knew, but Abaye came to him and restored it all to him. That is why you will frequently find it stated that Rabbi Joseph said. "I have not heard this law," and Abaye reminded him: "You, yourself, did teach it to us and did deduce it from such and such a teaching of the early sages."

A similar story is told about Rabbi Judah Hanasi. Although he had studied his teachings with thirteen different interpretations, he taught only seven of them to Rabbi Hiyya. When Rabbi Judah Hanasi fell sick, he forgot all his learning. Thereupon, Rabbi Hiyya restored to him the seven versions which had been taught him, but the other six were lost.

Now it happened that there was a certain workman who, while he cleaned and thickened his cloth, used to hear Rabbi Judah Hanasi when he was studying and going over his interpretations. So Rabbi Hiyya went and learned the remaining six versions from the workman and taught them once again to Rabbi Judah Hanasi. When the great Rabbi Judah Hanasi met the poor workman, he said to him: "You have taught both Rabbi Hiyya and me."

Rabbi Alexandri said that Rabbi Hiyya bar Abba had taught: Greater is the miracle performed for the sick than the one performed for Hananiah, Michael and Azariah when Nebuchadnezzar threw them into a fiery furnace. The miracle done for them concerned a fire kindled by man, which anyone might extinguish, but the recovery of the sick involves a heavenly fire and who can extinguish that?

Rabbi Alexandri also said that Rabbi Hiyya bar Abba (others say: Rabbi Joshua ben Levi) had taught: When a man's appointed end has come, all things have dominion over him. As Cain said of himself: *And it will be that whoever finds me will slay me.*

Rab deduced the same teaching from the verse: *They stand forth this day to receive Thy judgments; for all are Thy servants.* So too Samuel once saw a scorpion being carried across a river by a frog. Since scorpions cannot swim, the sight intrigued him. When it was on the other side, the scorpion stung a certain man so that he died. Thereupon Samuel quoted the verse: *They stand forth this day to receive Thy judgments; for all are Thy servants.*

Samuel said: Only a sick person who is feverish may be visited. Thus, one may not visit one with bowel trouble, eye disease, or headaches. The reason for excluding cases of bowel trouble is obvious. One should not cause embarrassment. The reason for the other two cases is in keeping with Rabbi Judah's dictum: "Speech is injurious to the eyes and to those suffering from headaches." (Many texts add: "But speech is good for fever.")

Raba said that if a fever were not a forerunner of the Angel of Death it would be good for a person to have a fever once every thirty days. Such a fever would be as salutary as the thorns which surround and protect a palm tree and as *theriak* (a poison antidote) is to the body. Rabbi Nahman ben Isaac said: "I want neither fever nor its *theriak!*"

5

Educating Children

A rabbinic legend tells of a group of non-Jews who once asked a heathen philosopher: "How can we do away with this Jewish people?" His answer was: "Go, observe their schools. As long as the voices of children ring forth from them, you will not be able to touch a hair of their heads. For thus have the Jews been promised by the father of their race: *'The voice is the voice of Jacob but the hands are the hands of Esau'* (*Genesis 27:22*). While the voice of Jacob resounds in the schools and academies, the hands of Esau have no power over him."

The Rabbis understood that the fate of the Jewish people is determined by their schools. The same concern persists today, aggravated by the fact that, in the opinion of most, the schooling provided Jewish youngsters is far from adequate.

While more and more Jewish children do receive some kind of formal religious training, their education generally ceases at the primary level. This is hardly adequate to gain a real comprehension of the complexities of Judaism, which are better grasped by a mature mind than by a child. There are those who insist that only a day-school education can provide Jewish youth with the in-depth knowledge of the Bible, Talmud and later Jewish writings that is required. Yet most Jewish parents do not wish to withdraw their children from public schools to enroll them in private Jewish schools.

This poses a dilemma. Jewish tradition has always held parents responsible for their children's education. They not only are expected to be examples but originally they were the instructors. When later parents employed others in this role, it was customary for them regularly to test their children to make certain that they were making proper progress. But most parents today do not lead their children in Jewishness; rather they tag along as best they can even though they do want their children to be Jews. The problem seems to center on making parents realize that their children's Jewishness hinges mostly on their own Jewishness, and that, in turn, is fundamentally a matter of self-education and determination.

Every Jew must therefore be concerned to measure himself against the standards set by the Jewish tradition. For the duty to educate one's children is not an imaginary ideal of spiritual leaders. It is incorporated into Jewish law and regularized by Jewish practice which can be traced back for nearly two thousand years.

The relevant regulations are summarized in the famous code of Jewish law published in 1567 called *Shulhan Arukh* (*The Prepared Table*). This work was composed by Rabbi Joseph Karo (1488–1575) to enable the Jew of modest learning to locate the relevant laws without having to make his way through the various Talmudic discussions and their later developments. The *Shulhan Arukh* became universally accepted as the authoritative guide to Jewish religious life and remains the basic code of traditional Jewish law to this day.

In the middle of the last century, Solomon Ganzfried (1804–1866), a Hungarian scholar, made an abridgment of the code which he called *Kitzur Shulhan Arukh* (*The Abbreviated Shulhan Arukh*), which presents the fundamental laws (in simple terms). Ganzfried's work has had wide circulation since its publication and remains a reliable, if brief, compilation of authentic tradition. What follows is his statement on the education of children.

FROM

Kitzur Shulhan Arukh

(*Section IV, Chapter 165*)

1. It is the duty of every father to train his children in the practice of all the precepts, both those of the Torah and those of the Rabbis. And to guard his children from any forbidden act, the child should be instructed in accordance with his or her intelligence, as the Scriptures say: *Train a child in the way he should go.* If words are of no avail, the father should punish the child physically. However, he should not strike him mercilessly as some fools do, but act intelligently. The father should take special care to train his children to tell no lies but to tell the truth at all times and to avoid swearing. All of these things are obligatory upon fathers as well as upon teachers.

2. The time for training a child in the performance of positive commandments depends upon the ability and the understanding of each child. Thus, as soon as the child understands the significance of the Sabbath, it becomes the child's duty to hear the blessing over the wine, the *kiddush,* the ceremony concluding the Sabbath, *havdalah,* and the like. The time to train a child to observe the negative commandments, whether Biblical or rabbinical, is when he or she understands when told that it is forbidden to do this or eat that. It is well to train a child to respond "Amen" and to give the other responses when at the synagogue. From the time that an infant begins to respond "Amen," he has a share in the world-to-come. It is important that children be trained to behave at the synagogue with awe and reverence. Children who run about to and fro and cause confusion should be kept home.

3. Even one who is not the child's father is forbidden to give him forbidden food or bid him do a forbidden act. According to

most authorities, it is forbidden to give him such food or to tell him to perform an act even when that act or food is forbidden only by a rabbinic ordinance rather than one stated in the Torah itself. If the child is somewhat ill and it is necessary for him to eat forbidden food, he may be fed by a non-Jew with food which is forbidden only by rabbinic law.

4. Not included in the precepts in which a child should be trained is a thing which is not forbidden in itself but is forbidden because of the nature of the day. Thus, it is therefore permissible to feed a child food on the Sabbath before the *kiddush* has been recited, although he must be trained to hear the *kiddush*. It is forbidden, however, to let a child eat outside the *sukkah,* the booth erected during the Feast of Tabernacles; for it is only in matters like eating before the *kiddush,* which partake of the nature of a negative command, that the law has been relaxed; but, whenever the clear violation of a positive command is involved, it is forbidden to let the child trangress it.

5. It is forbidden to tell a child, even if he is under the age of nine, to carry anything on the Sabbath, even for the purpose of fulfilling a precept, such as taking a prayerbook or a Bible to the synagogue.

6. If a minor steals anything, the stolen article should be returned if it is still intact. However, if it is no longer intact, he is not required to make restitution even after he becomes of age. But, to be justified in the sight of heaven, he should make restitution after reaching his majority. Likewise, if he had committed any other sin in his minority, then when he reaches the age of discernment it is well that he take upon himself to do a certain act as penance. Concerning this it is written: *That the soul be without knowledge is not good.*

7. A parent should not threaten a child with future punishment. If he sees him misbehave, he should either punish him at once or ignore the act. It is told in the Talmud that a certain child ran away from school and his father threatened him with punishment. The child thereupon committed suicide. Said the Rabbis of blessed memory: "In dealing with one's desire, with a child and with a woman, the left hand should repel and the

right hand should draw close." A parent should not frighten a child by means of profane threats or curses.

8. Legally, a Jewish child may be given to a non-Jewess to be nursed. Nevertheless, if it is possible to have it nursed by a Jewess, it should not be given to a non-Jewess. If a Jewish nurse must eat forbidden food as a remedy for some affliction she has, she should not nurse a child during those days, if possible.

9. Every father is obligated to teach the Torah to his son, for it is written: *And you shall teach them to your children to speak of them.* And just as he is obliged to teach his children, he is obliged to teach his grandchildren, as it is written: *And you shall make them known to your children and to your children's children.*

10. As soon as a child begins to talk, his father should teach him the verses: *Moses commanded us the Torah* and *Hear, O Israel, the Lord is our God, the Lord is One.* (However, one must be exceedingly careful to make certain that the child is clean while being taught.) He should likewise teach him some other verses little by little, until he is fit to attend school. At that time, the father should engage a teacher who is God-fearing, so that he may train the child to be God-fearing from his very youth. When the child has advanced to the study of the Scriptures, it is customary to begin to teach him the Book of Leviticus, which contains the laws of sacrifices and purification. For the Rabbis, of blessed memory, said: "Let the pure (i.e. the children) come and engage in the study of purity."

11. The teacher must teach the children the whole day and part of the night, so as to train them to study the Torah by day and by night. Under no circumstances should he interrupt their study, excepting at the close of the day preceding the Sabbath or a festival. Children should not be disturbed from their studies even for the purpose of rebuilding the Temple in Jerusalem.

12. A teacher who leaves the children to themselves and goes out, or engages in some other work, or who teaches carelessly, is included in: "Cursed be he who does the work of the Lord with a slack hand." Therefore, the teacher appointed should be a God-fearing man who can read fluently and grammatically. A

teacher should not stay awake at night up to a late hour, in order that he may not be languid while teaching. He should not fast or eat too sparingly. Nor should he eat or drink to excess, for all these things render him unfit to teach efficiently. A teacher who deviates from these rules forfeits his rights and should be dismissed.

13. A teacher should not punish the pupils like an enemy, with malice and cruelty, nor with a whip or a stick, but with a light strap.

14. On the Sabbath, a teacher should not teach the children a new lesson, because it is a burdensome activity on the Sabbath; but he may review with them a lesson they had learned previously.

15. It is forbidden to rob a minor of anything he has found and especially of something that was given to him as a gift.

16. A Jewish child should not be given to a pagan to be instructed in reading and writing or to be taught a trade, and needless to add that he should not be given to a heretical Jew, who is much worse than a pagan, for it is to be feared that the child will follow in his footsteps.

6

Preserving Life

There is much talk today of "situation ethics," of knowing right from wrong not by rule but by facing the circumstances in which one finds oneself and then determining the right. That seems to be more flexible and more desirable than a life based on law. Yet it may lead to license, to no real standards at all. *Halakhah* has its own form of flexibility; it works by careful analysis of specific cases and by insisting that some values are more important than others. Great scholars over the centuries were by these and other means able to adapt the law to changing circumstances.

The Sabbath laws, which are among the most seriously regarded in *halakhah,* with every safeguard invoked to prevent even a chance transgression, provide a pertinent illustration. Once it becomes necessary to save a life, the Sabbath can and must be violated. As the Rabbis ruled: "The saving of life takes precedence over the Sabbath." This general rabbinic attitude is based on the verse: *You shall therefore keep My statutes and ordinances and live by them. Halakhah* is given to enhance life and, when death may result from observing it, the law is waived. There are only three commandments which one should die rather than transgress: idolatry, sexual immorality and murder. Rabbi Ishmael was even prepared to concede in the case of idolatry in order to save life as long as it was done in private and not in public.

Two further examples demonstrate this Jewish commitment to life. Circumcision, basic to the Jewish religion, is clearly set forth in the Torah as a practice going back to the very beginnings of the Jews, the times of Abraham and Isaac. The ritual must take place exactly on the eighth day after birth, a timing of such importance that it supersedes the laws for observing the Sabbath. However, if the physician declares that circumcision on the eighth day would be injurious to the infant's health, the child may be "brought into the covenant of Abraham" with full religious sanction later, whenever his condition permits.

In the case of *kashrut,* a basic religious discipline for Jews, it is understood that a member of the Armed Services has no control over his diet. Where no reasonable alternative exists, a Jew in the Armed Services is permitted to eat non-kosher food.

The following passage discusses this principle as it applies to the Yom Kippur fast. It is taken from the Talmud, *Tractate Yoma* (literally: The Day, i.e. Yom Kippur), and treats of the duty of observing the Yom Kippur fast when a life may be at stake. In this instance, we are able to present the entire Mishnah and Gemara* text, thus offering a full sample of Talmudic literature. The passage is strictly legal, seeking to define the exact circumstances of a case where one may or may not eat. In so doing, it examines the meaning of the Mishnah text minutely, raising several problems concerning it and ending with a difference of opinion. Here is the Jewish approach to "situation ethics."

Yet the intent of the discussion is clear. Where life is at stake, the Yom Kippur law is waived—so says the law itself.

FROM

Talmud

(*Tractate Yoma, 82a–83a*)

MISHNAH: If, on Yom Kippur, a pregnant woman smells some food and craves for it greatly, she should be given a little until she no longer feels weak or faint; a sick person, too, is fed at

* The Mishnah, as noted previously, codifies the traditions of Jewish law as they had developed to about 200 C.E. The Gemara discussions which follow in the Talmud represent a selection of the comments about this Mishnah text made over the years until about 500 C.E.

the word of physicians. If no physicians are present, one feeds the sick person when he wants it—until he says: "Enough!"

GEMARA: Our Rabbis taught: If, on Yom Kippur, a pregnant woman smells the flesh of meat forbidden to her or of pork, we put a straw into the gravy in which it is cooking and place the other end in her mouth. If that satisfies her craving, it is well. If it does not, then she should be given the gravy itself. If that satisfies her craving, it is well. If it does not, then she should be given the meat itself. There is nothing that takes precedence over the duty to preserve life except the laws prohibiting idolatry, sexual immorality, and murder.

Where are we taught this about idolatry? There is a tradition that Rabbi Eliezer said: "Since the Torah said *With all thy soul,* why did it say *With all thy might?* Or, the question can be put in the reverse: since the Torah said *with all thy might,* why did it say: *with all thy soul?* The answer is: if there be a man whose life is dearer to him than his money (that is, "his might"), for him the Torah specifies: *Love God with all thy soul;* and if there be a person to whom his money is dearer than his life, for him too the Torah specifies: *Love God with all thy might.* With whatever is dearest him is he commanded to serve God.

Where are we taught this about sexual immorality and murder? Raba derived it from: *For as when a man rises against his neighbor and slays him, so is this matter, the rape of a betrothed maiden.* What can we infer from the punishment for raping a betrothed maiden that applies to a murderer?

This passage about the rapist teaches us something about murderers, and as a result something about rapists is learned. On the one hand, just as in the case of the betrothed maiden, it is lawful to save her even if it means killing the would-be raper, thus also in the case of a murderer. We may kill him to prevent his committing murder. On the other hand, just as in the case when one is ordered to commit murder, one should allow himself to be killed rather than transgress the command *you shall not murder,* thus also in the case of a command to rape a betrothed maiden, one should allow oneself to be killed rather than transgress the prohibition of violating her.

But, just how do we know that this principle of being killed rather than killing applies in the case when one is ordered to murder? That is simply logical, as in this tale: There was man who came before Raba and said to him: "The lord of my village told me: 'Kill so-and-so; if you will not, I will kill you.' What shall I do?" Raba answered: "Let him kill you but do not murder! What makes you think that your blood is redder than his? Perhaps his blood is redder than yours!"

There was once a pregnant woman who had smelled some food that was being cooked. Some people came to Rabbi Judah Hanasi to ask him what to do. He said to them: "Go and whisper to her that this is the Day of Atonement." They did this and she accepted the implication of the whispered suggestion. Thereupon Rabbi Judah applied to her in praise the verse describing the prophet Jeremiah: *Before I formed you in the womb, I knew you.* This woman gave birth to the illustrious Rabbi Yohanan.

On another occasion, a pregnant woman smelled some food that was being cooked. Some people came to Rabbi Hanina who similarly said to them: "Whisper to her that this is Yom Kippur." She did not accept the whispered suggestion. He cited this verse in regard to her: *The wicked are estranged from the womb.* She gave birth to Shabbatai, the notorious food speculator.

Concerning the phrase in the Mishnah passage: "A sick person is fed at the word of physicians," Rabbi Yannai said: "If the patient says: 'I need food,' and the doctor says: 'He does not need food'—we do what the patient says. What is the reason? As the Torah teaches: *The heart knows its own bitterness.* Is that not self-evident? No. You might have said: 'The physician knows better.' That is why the rule is that we do as the patient wishes. If the physician says: 'He needs it,' and the patient says that he does not, we do what the physician says. Why? We reason that a stupor must have seized the patient and he does not realize that he needs food."

Does not the statement: "A sick person is fed at the word of physicians" clearly imply that the patient is fed only upon the order of physicians but not at his own word, thus refuting the interpretation of Rabbi Yannai? No. The literal wording refers only to the case when the patient says: "I do not need it." Then we feed him on the advice of the physicians.

A question remains: it says "physicians." Should one feed him upon the order of only one doctor? Normally yes, but the plural wording of the Mishnah text refers to a case when someone else is present who agrees with the patient that he does not need food. If that is so, why bother stating that the patient is "fed at the word of physicians?" Surely, that is self-evident, for there is the possibility of danger to human life and there is a well-known legal principle that "in the case of the possibility of danger to human life we take a more lenient view." *

It must be said this way in order to include a case in which two more people (making three now) are present who say that he does not need to be fed. Despite their being outnumbered, the word of two physicians is decisive. That is true even though Rabbi Safra said that the ruling: "Two are as a hundred and a hundred as two" applies only to actual witnesses to a case, but with regard to matters of opinion we go according to the majority of opinions. Rabbi Safra's ruling about the majority of expert opinions applies only to cases of money matters. Here, the case is one which involves the possibility of danger to human life and we take the lenient view even against a majority of opinions.

Since, in the second part of the Mishnah, it states: "And if no physicians are there, one feeds him at his own wish," is it to be inferred that the first part deals with the case when he said he needed food and thus refutes all the previous reasoning? No. The Mishnah text is incomplete and this is how it should read: "The previous stipulations apply only for the case when he says: 'I do not need food'; but, if he says: 'I need food,' then if two physicians are not there but only one who says: 'He does not need it,' then, despite the one physician's view, one feeds him at his own wish."

Mar, the son of Rab Ashi, said: "Whenever he says: 'I need food,' even if there be a hundred who say: 'He does not need it,' we accept his statement, as it is said: *The heart knows*

* See *Tractate Shabbat,* 129a.

its own bitterness. We learned this in the Mishnah: 'If no physicians are there, one feeds him at his own wish.' That means only if no physicians were present, but what if there were dissenting physicians present? This is what is meant: The previous stipulations of the Mishnah apply only for the case when he says: 'I do not need food,' but if he says: 'I need food,' then we do not reckon with any physician's opinion at all but feed him at his own wish, as it said: *The heart knows its own bitterness.*"

III

BELONGING TO THE JEWISH PEOPLE

In an age of expanding internationalism, nationalism remains a vital political force. Mankind faces the critical problem of how to maintain simultaneous loyalty to one's own group and to all of mankind.

Judaism's experience in this area has been unique. Being both a folk and a faith, a particular people imbued with a universal vision, it embraces both positions. Jews have a primary duty to foster the welfare of their people, Israel, but through it to serve all humanity. The roots come first. Judaism encourages a "we" feeling which embraces a long and varied history and which reaches out to Jews wherever they may be scattered. The weekly Sabbath afternoon prayer quotes the Torah: "You God are One and Your Name is One; and who is like Your people Israel, unique on earth?"

Yet this love of the Jewish people is directed toward a Messianic future of international human brotherhood. If God is the Father of all men, then all men must live as brothers. In the Book of Isaiah the Messianic vision is given its classic expression:

> Nation shall not lift up sword against nation,
> Neither shall they learn war any more.
>
> (2:4)

Neither here nor in the other prophetic visions is the disappearance of separate nations envisioned. The prophets, thinking of the Kingdom of God on earth, saw nations as a legitimate human expression though they believed they needed to learn how to live together under God's own rule. Though no more inherently evil than family life, nationality, being infused with vast power, has been difficult to sanctify. For Judaism peoplehood is regarded as a means of achieving universal brotherhood.

The Prayerbook often expresses these yearnings of the Jewish people in its own behalf as well as on behalf of all mankind. The *Aleinu,* the Adoration, which regularly concludes Jewish worship, speaks of the uniqueness of the Jewish people in its first paragraph and, in the second, relates this to all peoples coming to serve God. The ritual for the blowing of the *shofar,* the ram's horn, on the High Holy Days speaks of its particular meaning as having been sounded at Sinai and its universal meaning as ultimately proclaiming the advent of the Messiah. For the Jew, the more truly Jewish he is, the more human he becomes; the deeper his Jewish roots, the greater his humanitarian outreach.

In recent times some modern Jews have not always perceived this truth. They have been so eager to take advantage of the benefits of Western civilization from which they are no longer excluded, as their fathers had been for nearly fifteen centuries, that they have rushed to abandon their heritage as a way of securing their status in the new world. Assimilation, however, has proved self-defeating. It weakens both the individual and the group. The individual becomes uprooted and insecure; the group is less able to contribute its unique style of life and standards to all mankind.

Self-respect does not, however, mean the polar opposite—that to fulfill his obligation to the people of Israel every Jew must move to the State of Israel. To be sure, there have been and will be many who do immigrate, if not out of political necessity, out of a desire to live fully in a Jewish culture. However, as experience teaches, most choose to remain in the democratic lands where they are citizens. Their spiritual and cultural loyalties to their fellow Jews are not limited by geography or prior political loyalty to the countries where they reside. The responsibility to be true to the Jewish people remains an important part of every Jew's outlook.

This modern Jewish concern with the State of Israel has old Jewish roots. Throughout the long years of homelessness and deprivation, the Jewish people never ceased to long for its ancestral homeland, for the Zion of the patriarchs, prophets and sages. On weekdays and Sabbaths, at birth and at death, in word and in thought, *Eretz Yisrael,* the Land of Israel, has been remembered. Jews never surrendered their faith in their people's ultimate return to its soil. The traditional love for the Promised Land received fresh impetus with the birth of modern political Zionism, the establishment of the State of Israel, and the subsequent threats to its continued existence.

This may seem a "secular" concern. But Jews are more than a religious communion or a creedal association, a biological race or a political nation. They are a religious people, a God-covenanted people. That is why they fuse peoplehood and humanhood into one way of life. That is why their bonds of kinship are richer than those binding a faith-community. Jewish mutuality is based not only on a shared history and culture but on a feeling of common destiny. The aware Jew knows that whatever affects one segment of his people affects all Jews and ultimately all mankind.

7

Loving the Land

In 1948 the State of Israel was born. Whatever individual Diaspora Jews may have felt about Zionism prior to that historic event, nearly all rejoiced that the State came into existence, and have since expressed concern for its welfare and upbuilding. Though Jews outside Israel, particularly in the United States, have been generous in their support of the new state, membership has radically decreased in the Zionist organizations which were so important to its establishment.

This present-day organizational difficulty is rooted in a more subtle philosophical issue. The historic love of Jews for *Eretz Yisrael* is clear to anyone who examines the record. The Prayerbook, the book closest to every Jew regardless of status or scholarship, repeatedly refers to the hope for the restoration of Zion. About a hundred years ago the Reform Prayerbook eliminated these prayers as casting unnecessary doubt upon Jewish loyalty to the countries in which Jews had just been granted the rights of citizenship.

While that problem now seems far behind us, it is not easy to identify the modern secular State of Israel with the restored Messianic Zion for which the Jewish people has so long prayed and hoped. The relationship between Jews and Israel and those who live elsewhere remains a live issue today.

There is not to be found in Jewish tradition any treatment of the reality of a modern, democratic state wherein Jews constitute the majority. When it stresses the duty of the Jew to love Zion and the Land of Israel, however, it touches on the root from which that concern arises. Perhaps the most eloquent exponent of this was the great poet of Spanish Jewry, Yehudah Halevi (c.1086–c.1145), whose poems are recognized as one of the great glories of the Golden Age. His verses dealing with love of God were absorbed into the liturgy, while his odes to the Jewish people have been transmitted as a powerful expression of Jewish hope and aspiration.

Halevi's major philosophic work is *The Kuzari,* an examination of the Jewish soul with the help of logic: its subtitle is "The Book of Argument and Demonstration in Aid of the Despised Faith."

The setting is the court of the Khazars, a Slavic people whose royal house converted to Judaism in the eighth century. The book opens with King Bulan's search for religious truth by listening to the presentations of a philosopher, a Catholic priest, a Moslem imam. After these prove unsatisfactory, the king of the Khazars engages in a dialogue with a rabbi—which makes up the balance of the work. In his exposition of Judaism, which ultimately wins the king as a convert, the rabbi, who is the author's mouthpiece, asserts that the Jews are to the rest of the world what the heart is to the body: Israel is God's instrument for the religious education of mankind. The Jews therefore owe it to themselves and humanity to be what they were designed to be: a prophetic people. However, they cannot completely fulfill their destiny as a people on alien soil; that can be done only in one place, in the Promised Land.

FROM

The Kuzari

(Part II, Sections 10–24)

BY YEHUDAH HALEVI

RABBI: You may easily perceive that one country can have qualities that another does not. For example, certain plants or minerals or animals are found in one specific place and not elsewhere or the inhabitants of one land have certain traits or appearances different from those in another.

KING: But I never heard that the inhabitants of Palestine were more distinguished than others.

RABBI: Think of the hill on which you say that the vines thrive so well—if it has not been properly tended and cultivated, grapes would not have been produced. So, it is necessary first to consider the original people, and second the religious events that occurred there. This can be compared to the cultivation of the vineyard. Just as no other hill can produce such wine, no other land can share the distinction of the divine influence.

KING: Is this so? Were not prophetic visions granted to Abraham in Ur, and to Ezekiel and Daniel in Babylon, and to Jeremiah in Egypt, all outside the Land of Israel?

RABBI: Whoever prophesied was either in the Holy Land or else the prophecy was about the Holy Land, e.g. Abraham's message was to go there and the others' were about the Land. Moreover, Ezekiel and Daniel lived during the time of the First Temple and thus had a direct contact with the divine which, because they were duly prepared, enabled them to prophesy.

Adam too lived and died in the Land, for tradition tells us that Adam and Eve as well as the patriarchs and their wives were buried there. This is the land which the Bible says is *before the Lord* and which *the eyes of the Lord are always upon*. It was also the first object of jealousy between Cain and Abel, who wanted to know which of them would be their father's heir, inherit that land, and thus be in direct contact with God, while the other, bereft of it, would be a nonentity. Then, Abel was killed by Cain and there was no heir. For it is stated that Cain went out of the presence of the Lord, which means that he left the Land, as it is written: *Behold, You have driven me out this day from being upon the Land and from Your face shall I be hid.*

That too is the implication of: *But Jonah rose up to flee unto Tarshish, from the presence of the Lord,* which means he was fleeing the land of prophecy. God, however, brought him back to the Land of Israel in the belly of the fish and appointed him a prophet in the land to prophesy in Nineveh . . .

Did not Abraham, after having had contact with the divine, move from Ur, his city, to the Land where his perfection could become complete? This is like a farmer who finds the root of a good tree in a wilderness. He transplants it into properly tilled ground to enable it to grow, to change it from a wild root into a cultivated one, from one which bore fruit only by chance to one which produces a luxuriant crop.

In the same way, the gift of prophecy was retained by Abraham's descendants in the Land as long as they fulfilled the required conditions to prepare themselves: purity, worship, sacrifices, and, above all, reverence of the Divine Presence . . .

KING: Continue your discourse on the special advantages of the Land of Israel.

RABBI: It was appointed to guide the world and, from early days, was assigned to the tribes of Israel. Abraham did not come completely under the divine influence nor enter into a covenant with God until he came thither . . . It was so holy that the Land itself was given Sabbaths, the Sabbatical years, as it is said: *Shabbat* of the Land, and *The Land shall keep a* Shabbat *unto the Lord.* It is forbidden to sell it forever, as it is said: *For Mine is the Land.* Observe that the "feasts of the Lord" and the "Sabbaths of the Land" belong to the "Land of the Lord."

KING: Was not the day primarily calculated as dawning first in China, because it forms the eastern beginning of the inhabited earth?

RABBI: The beginning of the Sabbath must be calculated from Sinai.* The Sabbath does not begin until the sun has set behind Sinai, and so on to the remote west and around the

* This passage is one of the classic sources used in discussing the Jewish calendar equivalent of the International Date Line.

world to China which is at the extreme end of the inhabited earth. The Sabbath begins in China eighteen hours later than in the Land of Israel which lies in the center of the world . . .

It was in that land that the law was given and where Adam, at the end of the Sabbath, was transferred from the Garden. It is there that the calendar began after the six days of creation . . . It would be impossible for the days of the week to have the same names all over the world unless, for purposes of keeping a calendar, we fix one place which marks the beginning of days and another one not far off . . . the one should be east absolutely and the other west absolutely.

If this were not so, the days could not have definite names and every point of the equator would be east and west at the same time. China would thus be east for the Land of Israel but west for the other side. There would be neither east nor west, neither beginning nor end, nor definite names for the days. Adam, however, did give definite names to the days, taking the Land as his starting point . . .

Thus, knowledge of the "Sabbath of the Lord" and of the "Festivals of the Lord" depends on the Land which is the "inheritance of the Lord" and is also called "His holy mountain," "His footstool," and "gate of heaven." You know how the patriarchs lived in the country even when it was in the hands of pagans, how they yearned for it, and, like Jacob and Joseph, had their bodies carried to it.

Moses prayed to see it, and when this was denied to him, considered it a misfortune. Therefore, it was shown to him from the top of Mt. Pisgah as an act of grace. Persians, Indians, Greeks and others begged to be allowed to offer up sacrifices and to be prayed for in the Holy Temple; they spent their wealth there, even though they believed in other laws rather than in the Torah.

To this day, they honor it even though the Divine Presence is no longer revealed there. All nations, longing for it, make pilgrimages to it, except for us because we are punished and in disgrace. All that the Rabbis tell of its great qualities would take too long to relate.

KING: Let me hear a few of their observations.

RABBI: One statement is: "All roads lead up to the Land of Israel, but none from it." A woman who refuses to accompany her husband there should be divorced and she forfeits her dower rights. On the other hand, if the husband refuses to accompany his wife thither, he may be forced to divorce her and must pay her the marriage settlement.

The Rabbis also say: It is better to dwell in the Holy Land, even in a town mostly inhabited by heathens, than abroad in a town full of Jews. He who dwells in the Holy Land is compared to one who has a God, and he who lives elsewhere to one who has no God. David's statement: *For they have driven me out this day from abiding in the inheritance of the Lord, saying: "Go, serve other gods"* is cited as a proof that he who lives outside the Land may be considered like one who serves strange gods.

Another saying is: To be buried in the Land of Israel is like being buried beneath the Temple altar. The sages praise him who lives in the Land more than one who is carried there dead. This is expressed in this way: He who embraces it alive is not like him who does so after his death. They say concerning one who could live there but did not, and only ordered his body to be taken there after death: "While you lived, you made My inheritance an abomination, but in death you come and contaminate My country."

It is told that Rabbi Hananya, when asked whether it was lawful to go abroad to marry one's brother's widow, said: "His brother married a pagan woman; praised be God who caused him to die. Now this one follows him!" The sages also forbade selling estates or the remains of a house there to a heathen or leaving such a house in ruins. Other sayings are: "Fines can only be imposed in the Land itself"; "No slave may be shipped from the Land abroad"; "The very air of the Holy Land makes one wise." They expressed their love of the Land as follows: "He who walks four cubits in the Land of Israel is assured of happiness in the world-to-come." A heathen criticized Rabbi Zera for his foolhardiness in crossing a river without waiting to reach a ford out of eagerness to enter the Land. Rabbi Zera replied: "The place which not even Moses and Aaron were privileged to reach cannot be reached speedily enough by me!"

KING: If this is so, even though you pray: "Have mercy on Zion" and believe that the Divine Presence will return there, you are remiss in your duty by not striving to reach that place and making it your home in life and death. The fact that the Divine Presence dwelt there for five hundred years is enough reason to go there and to find that purification attainable where the prophets and the pious lived.

Is it not "the gate of heaven?" All nations agree on this point. Islam teaches that it is the place where Mohammed ascended on high, that prophets go up to heaven from there, and that it is the place of gathering on the day of resurrection. Everybody turns to it in prayer and visits it on a pilgrimage. Your forefathers chose that land in preference to their birthplaces and lived there as strangers even though they were surrounded by idolatry and impurity. But they had no other desire than to remain. Even in times of famine they left only with God's permission. And they directed that their bones be interred there.

RABBI: This is a severe reproach, O King of the Khazars! During the Babylonian exile, this was the sin which prevented fulfillment of the promise: *Sing and rejoice, O daughter of Zion.* If only the people in exile had agreed to return, everything would have been restored as it had been.

But only certain individuals were ready to do so; the majority and the aristocracy remained in Babylonia, preferring slavery as long as they did not have to leave their homes and their businesses . . . Were we prepared to meet the God of our forefathers with a pure mind, we should find the same salvation as did our fathers when they were in Egypt.

(*Part V, Sections 23–28*)

RABBI: The Land of Israel is especially distinguished by the Lord of Israel, and no function can be perfect except there. Many of the Israelite laws do not apply to those who do not live there. The heart and soul are completely pure only in the place believed to be specially selected by God . . .

This sacred place serves to remind men and to stimulate them to love God, which is both a reward and a promise, as it is written: *You will arise and have mercy on Zion, for the time to favor her, the set time, is come. Your servants take pleasure in her stones and embrace the dust thereof.* This means that Jerusalem can be rebuilt only when Israel yearns for it to such an extent that they embrace her stones and dust.

KING: If this be so, it would be a sin to hinder you in your desire to go there. To the contrary, it is meritorious to help you. May God give you His help and be your protector and friend. May He favor you with His mercy.

8

Being True to the Jewish People

Until the French Revolution, both Jew and non-Jew regarded the Jewish people as a religious nation in exile. Once the Jews were admitted into citizenship in their respective countries, however, their peoplehood became an embarrassment.

Many Jews began to argue that the bond between Jews was purely religious, making full citizenship possible for Jews but also allowing those who did not observe the tenets and rituals of Judaism to feel free to drop their Jewish ties. Some sought to secure their newly gained freedom by becoming as much like their non-Jewish neighbors as possible. Others spurned their Jewishness, even to the point of identifying themselves with the prejudices of the non-Jewish world. As the nineteenth century passed into the twentieth, this process of conscious assimilation and Jewish defection quickened.

Today, most Jews understand the sickness of self-hatred. They tend to recognize that turning against one's brothers and against what is Jewish in oneself grows out of a desire, conscious or unconscious, to identify with the non-Jewish world.

There is also a growing acceptance in the world at large of human difference, of the fact that everyone must not necessarily conform to the white Anglo-Saxon Protestant style. In the United States, Jews, like the Irish and the Italians, the many Catholics and the few Buddhists, have loyalties beyond that which they owe their country. This very "extra" provides them with something special to contribute to the United States.

The effects of Jewish self-hatred are immediately recognizable: avoiding situations which will remind others of one's Jewishness; being uncomfortable with expressions of Judaism and preferring that one's Jewish associations be as undistinctive as possible. Even well-adjusted Jews are affected to some degree by this sickness. Jewish aggressiveness and assertiveness are often only a compensation for what is at heart a sense of Jewish inferiority. It has even been suggested that the special tensions of Jewish life have been the source of Jewish Diaspora creativity these past two thousand years.

One of the most brilliant defenders of modern Jewish self-respect and self-determination was Ahad Ha-am (1856–1927). His real name was Asher Ginzberg but he was known throughout the Jewish world by his pen-name which means "one of the people." Born in Russia, he received a traditional Hebraic education and taught himself Western literature. For ten years he edited a Hebrew journal called *Hashiloah,* which soon became the standard for the then emerging Hebrew literature: clarity and simplicity of expression were stressed.

Appearing in the journal were Ahad Ha-am's own essays, which won him many disciples. For more than four decades he provided the most provocative and stimulating thinking about Jews and Judaism. Every reader of modern Hebrew knew his writings and discussed his ideas, which evolved into the distinct philosophy of "Cultural Zionism." Ahad Ha-am's principal thesis was that *Eretz Yisrael* must become the cultural-spiritual center of world Jewry, with quality never to be sacrificed for the sake of quantity. It was Ahad Ha-am's teachings that made Zionism a movement for educational and cultural creativity as well as for political and economic reconstruction. It was his central thesis that the revival of the Jewish nation must involve the revival of Judaism.

In *Avdut Betokh Herut* ("Slavery Amidst Freedom"), an essay written in 1891, Ahad Ha-am criticizes the historian Simon Dubnow's view that a certain volume of essays published in Paris reflected the fact that the Jews of Paris were living up to the eternal ideals of Judaism despite the prevalence of anti-Semitism. In Ahad Ha-am's view, the book rather reflected the desperate anxiety of French Jews to show that they were not really different from non-Jews. Thus, in a moral sense and despite their supposed political freedom, they were actually slaves to their majority culture, in contrast with the Jews from Eastern Europe who, though socially oppressed, were Jewish without self-consciousness, and therefore more truly free.

FROM

Slavery Amidst Freedom

BY AHAD HA-AM

I have before me a new French book called *La Gerbe*. It was issued last year to commemorate the fiftieth anniversary of the French journal, *Archives Israélites*. Had such a jubilee volume been published twenty years ago, it would undoubtedly have recounted with paeans of triumph all the victories of the "Frenchmen of the Jewish persuasion" during these fifty years.

But in fact it appears now and not twenty years ago, and what is it we hear? Cries of defeat, not paeans of triumph. It is in vain that we look for any sign of genuine rejoicing. Through the whole book, there runs an undercurrent of grief, a dark thread of lamentation.

Let us hear the editor himself. After stating that the Jews after 1789 possessed rights on paper but not in practice, he asks in a parenthesis: "Do they exist fully even in 1890?" He then goes on to recount his battles against prejudice and how he has tried unceasingly to spread the great principle of social assimilation. What he says amounts to this, that even the second jubilee after the principles of '89 has not brought the desired happiness; that hatred of the Jews has revived even in France despite the principles of '89 and despite all the battles against prejudice and all efforts to promote assimilation. And so—our respected editor promises to continue to fight and strive.

The writers in *La Gerbe* are distinguished and do not let others see that they are afraid. They know how to control themselves and make a show of looking at all these things from above; they know how to comfort themselves and their readers with pleasant hopes and fair promises, which read sometimes like little prophecies.

One of the writers promises us on his word that this is the last battle between the Jews and their enemies, and it will end in complete victory for us, to be followed by real peace for all time. The great Revolution of '89 is always on their tongues. They refer again and again to the "rights of man" (*les droits de l'homme*), or, as some put it, "the new Ten Commandments" which that Revolution promulgated; and each time they express the hope—a hope which is also a sort of prayer—that the French people will not forever forget those great days, that the French people will not, *cannot* turn back, that the French people is still, as of old, the great, the enlightened, the glorious, the mighty people, and so forth, and so forth.

Whether these prophecies will be fulfilled or not is a question with which we are not here concerned. But in the meantime it requires no very penetrating vision to discern from them, and from the pages of *La Gerbe* generally, the true spiritual condition of the French Jews at the present time. There is here none of that "exaltation" which some would fain discover, but the exact opposite. Their condition may be justly defined as spiritual slavery under the veil of outward freedom. In reality they accepted this slavery a hundred years ago, together with their "rights"; but it is only in these evil days that it stands revealed in all its "glory."

The writers of *La Gerbe* try, for instance, to prove to us and to our enemies that the fortunes of the Jews in every country are inextricably bound up with those of its other inhabitants, or even with those of humanity as a whole; that the troubles of the Jews in any particular country are not, therefore, peculiar to them, but are shared by all the other inhabitants, or even by humanity as a whole.

This trick of exciting sympathy with the Jews on the ground that it will benefit other people is very familiar to us here also. Our Russian Jewish writers are never weary of seeking arguments to prove that the Jews are a milch cow, which must be treated gently for the sake of its milk. Naturally, our French *savants* do not condescend to use this ugly metaphor. They wrap up the idea in a nice "ideal" form.

But when all is said, the idea is the same there as here; and a terrible idea it is, sufficient in itself to show how far even Western Jews are from being free men at heart. Picture the situation to yourself. Surrounded by armed bandits, I cry out "Help! Help! Danger!" Is not every man bound to hasten to my help? Is it not a fearful, an indelible disgrace, that I am forced to prove first of all that my danger affects other people, affects the whole human race? As though my blood were not good enough, unless it be mingled with the blood of others! As though the human race were something apart, in which I have no share, and not simply a collective name for its individual members, of whom I am one!

This slavery becomes more and more apparent, when the writers in *La Gerbe* come to deal with the internal affairs of Judaism. Valiantly they champion the cause of our religion against its rivals, knowing as they do that this is permitted in France, where neither the government nor the people cares very much about such discussions. But when they have to disclose the national connection between the Jews of France and other Jews, or between them and their ancestral land, a connection in which it is possible to find something inconsistent to a certain extent with the extreme and zealous patriotism which is in vogue in France, then we discover once more their moral slavery —a spiritual yoke which throttles them, and reduces them to a condition of undisguised embarrassment.

One of the contributors, the distinguished philosopher Adolphe Franck, expresses the opinion that every Jew, without distinction of nationality, who enjoys the fruits of emancipation in any country, is bound to be grateful, first and foremost, to the Frenchmen of the Revolution, and must therefore regard France as his first fatherland, the second being his actual birthplace.

And here our philosopher finds it his duty suddenly to add: "Jerusalem is (for the Jew) nothing more than the birthplace of his memories and his faith. He may give it a place in his religious service; but he himself belongs to the land of his birth." This way of regarding Jerusalem is a very trite commonplace, which our Western thinkers grind out again and again in various forms.

Not long ago another philosopher, a German Jew, published a new volume, which contains a scientific article on the Book of Lamentations. Now, a scientific article has no concern with questions of practical conduct; and yet the author finds it necessary to touch in conclusion on the practical question, whether at the present day we have a right to read this book in our synagogues. He answers in the affirmative, on the ground that the Christians too read it in their churches three days before Easter. "If we are asked, 'What is Zion to you, and what are you to Zion?' we reply calmly, 'Zion is the innermost kernel of the inner consciousness of modern nations.' " This answer is not perhaps so clear as it might be, even in the original; but the writer's object is perfectly clear. We have, therefore, no right to be angry if our French philosopher also adopts this view.

But when we read the whole article in *La Gerbe* and find the author concluding that the Jews have a special "mission," which they received *in Jerusalem,* which they have not yet completely fulfilled, and for the sake of which they live, and *must live* till they do fulfill it completely, then we shall have a serious question to put. The duty of gratitude, we argue, is so important in our author's view that he would have every Jew put France before the country of his birth. That country was nothing more than the cause of our obtaining external rights, which we might have obtained without her, if only we had deserted our "mission."

That being so, does it not follow *a fortiori* that Jerusalem, which gave us this very "mission," the cause and object of our life, has a claim on our gratitude prior even to that of France? Even so great a philosopher as our author could not, I think, find a logical flaw in this argument: and yet he could write as he has done. Is not this moral slavery?

But this moral slavery is only half the price which Western Jews have paid for their emancipation. Beneath the cloak of their political freedom there lies another, perhaps a harder, form of slavery—intellectual slavery; and this, too, has left its mark on the book which we are considering.

Having agreed, for the sake of emancipation, to deny the existence of the Jews as a people, and regard Judaism simply and solely as a religion, Western Jews have thereby pledged themselves and their posterity to guard with the utmost care the religious unity of Israel.

But emancipation demanded certain practical changes in religious matters; and everybody could make this sacrifice. Hence people "of the Jewish persuasion" have split into various sects; the unity of the religion, on its practical side, has vanished. There remains, then, no other bond than that of religion on its theoretical side—that is to say, certain abstract beliefs which are held by all Jews.

This bond, apart from the inherent weakness which it has in common with every spiritual conception that is not crystallized into practice, has grown still weaker of recent years, and is becoming more and more feeble every day. Scientific development has shaken the foundations of every faith, and the Jewish faith has not escaped; so much so that even the editor of *La Gerbe* confesses, with a sigh, that "the scientific heresy which bears the name of Darwin" is gaining ground, and it is only from a feeling of *noblesse oblige* that he still continues to combat it.

What, then, are those Jews to do who have nothing left but this theoretical religion, which is itself losing its hold on them? Are they to give up Judaism altogether, and become completely assimilated to their surroundings? A few of them have done this: but why should not they all adopt the same course? Why do most of them feel that they cannot? Where is the chain to which they can point as that which holds them fast to Judaism, and does not allow them to be free? Is it the instinctive national feeling which they have inherited, which is independent of religious beliefs and practices? Away with the suggestion! Did they not give up this feeling a hundred years ago, in exchange for emancipation?

Yet the fact remains that it is not in their power to uproot this feeling. Try as they will to conceal it, seek as they will for subterfuges to deceive the world and themselves, it lives none the less; resent it as they will, it is a force at the center of their being.

But this answer, though it satisfies us, does not satisfy them. They have publicly renounced their Jewish nationality, and they cannot go back on their words; they cannot confess that they have sold that which was not theirs to sell.

But this being so, how can they justify their obstinate clingings to the name of Jew—a name which brings them neither honor nor profit—for the sake of certain theoretical beliefs which they no longer hold, or which, if they do really and sincerely maintain them, they might equally hold without this special name, as every non-Jewish deist has done?

For a long time this question has been constantly troubling the Jewish thinkers of Western Europe; and it is this question which drove them, in the last generation, to propound that new, strange gospel to which they cling so tenaciously to this very day —I mean that famous gospel of "the mission of Israel among the nations."

This theory is based on an antiquated idea, which is at variance with all the principles of modern science, as though every nation had been created from the first for some particular purpose, and so had a "mission" which it must fulfill, living on against its will until its heaven-sent task is done. Thus, for example, the Greeks were created to polish and perfect external beauty; the Romans to exalt and extol physical force. On this hypothesis, it is not difficult to find an answer to our question—an answer not inconsistent, on the one hand, with emancipation, and, on the other hand, with the unity of Judaism.

The answer is this: Israel as a people is dead; but the Jewish Church still lives, and must live, because the mission of Israel is not completely fulfilled, so long as absolute monotheism, with all its consequences, has not conquered the whole world. Till that victory is achieved, Israel must live in spite of itself, must bear and suffer and fight: to this end it was created—"to know God and to bring others to that knowledge."

It is perhaps superfluous to deal at length with this theory, which, indeed, it is difficult, in our day, to treat seriously. We are forced, despite ourselves, into a smile, a smile of bitter irony, when we see distinguished men, who might have shown their sorely tried people real light on its hard and thorny path, wasting their time with such pleasant sophistries as these; trying to believe, and to persuade others, that a whole people can have maintained its existence, and borne a heavy burden of religious observance and an iron yoke of persecutions, torments and curses for thousands of years, all for the purpose of teaching the world a certain philosophy, which is already expounded in whole libraries of books, in every conceivable language and every conceivable style, from which he who will may learn without any assistance from us: and especially at the present time, when the number of those who wish to learn grows less every day, nay, when we ourselves are every day forgetting our own teaching.

It is, indeed, surprising that such a thinker as Munk, and even the older thinkers of our own day, could and still can believe in the mission of Israel in the sense explained above. But we shall be less surprised if we remember that Munk wrote in the "forties" and that the older contributors to *La Gerbe* are for the most part children of that earlier generation which educated them—children of an age in which the idea of a "final cause" was intelligible and current as a scientific theory.

It is, however, a strange phenomenon, and more difficult to explain, that the same position should be adopted by thinkers and writers of the present generation. These men, who know and admit that "the scientific heresy which bears the name of Darwin" is gaining ground, that is to say, that the world is accepting gradually a scientific theory which does not admit the existence of purpose or end even where it seems most obvious. How can these men still cling to a doctrine which demands belief in the missions of nations generally, in the mission of Israel in particular, and above all, in such a wonderful mission as this?

There can be but one answer. They are compelled to do so, because they can find no other way of reconciling Judaism with emancipation. In the first place, Israel has no right to be anything but a church consecrated to heaven; in the second place, this heavenly bond has become too weak; and in the third place—and this is the important thing—they feel, in spite of it all, that Jews they are, and Jews they want to be. And so, in order to conceal the contradiction between these "truths," they are forced to take refuge in this antiquated theory.

On all other questions of conduct or of scholarship they belong to their own generation; but on the Jewish question they cannot move from the position which their fathers took up fifty years ago. As though these fifty years had brought no change of idea and outlook into the world!

Thus this intellectual slavery also is a result of political freedom. If not for this freedom, emancipated Jews would not deny the existence of the Jewish nation; they would not have to climb up to heaven, on an old and rickety ladder, to seek there what they might have found on earth.

It might be maintained, indeed, that even then there would have been thinkers who inclined to look for some "mission" for their people, or, to speak more accurately, for some spiritual aim suited to its spiritual characteristics. But then they might have found a different aim—not, perhaps, a finer one, but still one that would have gained acceptance more readily, one more in accordance with the ideas of modern times and with the truths of logic and history.

For instance, they might have argued thus: Here our people has been wandering over the face of the earth for some two thousand years, in the course of which we do not find that it has ever consciously invented any new thing of importance, has ever beaten out any new highway on the tract of life. Its part has been always that of the huckster; it has peddled about all kinds of goods, material and spiritual, of other people's making. All the good work which the Jews did for the world's culture in the Middle Ages was at bottom nothing but huckstering and peddling: they picked up learning in the East, and gave it to the West.

"Yes," replies Munk, in extenuation, "because the mission of Israel does not lie in making new discoveries." Well, so let it be! But now that we see that Israel was fitted to be, and in fact has been, a huckster of culture, surely common sense will tell us that this is the occupation for Israel to follow now, if some spiritual aim is wanted. Now, therefore, that we have acquired culture in the West, let us return and carry it to the East. And, if we are so very fond of teaching, it is surely better for us to go where there is a more evident lack of teachers, and where it is easier to find attentive pupils.

But the truth is that if Western Jews were not slaves to their emancipation, it would never have entered their heads to consecrate their people to spiritual missions or aims before it had fulfilled that physical natural "mission" which belongs to every organism—before it had created for itself conditions suitable to its character, in which it could develop its latent powers and aptitudes, its own particular form of life, in a normal manner, and in obedience to the demands of its nature.

Then, and only then, we may well believe, its development might lead it in course of time to some field of work in which it would be specially fitted to act as teacher, and thus contribute once again to the general good of humanity, in a way suited to the spirit of the modern world. And if then philosophers tell us that in this field of work lies the "mission" of our people, for which it was created, I shall not, indeed, be able to subscribe to their view; but I shall not quarrel with them on a mere question of names.

But alas! I shall doubtless be dead and buried before then. Today, while I am still alive, I try to give my weary eyes a rest from the scene of ignorance, of degradation, of unutterable poverty that confronts me here in Russia, and find comfort by looking yonder across the border, where there are Jewish professors, Jewish members of academies, Jewish officers in the army, Jewish civil servants, and when I see there, behind the glory and the grandeur of it all, a twofold spiritual slavery—moral slavery and intellectual slavery—and ask myself: Do I envy these fellow-Jews of mine their emancipation?

I answer, in all truth and sincerity: No! a thousand times no! The privileges are not worth the price! I may not be emancipated; but at least I have not sold my soul for emancipation. I at least can proclaim from the housetops that my kith and kin are dear to me wherever they are, without being constrained to find forced and unsatisfactory excuses. I at least can remember Jerusalem at other times than those of "divine service": I can mourn for its loss, in public or in private, without being asked what Zion is to me, or I to Zion. I at least have no need to exalt my people to heaven, to trumpet its superiority above all other nations, in order to find a justification for its existence.

I at least know "why I remain a Jew"—rather, I can find no meaning in such a question, any more than if I were asked why I remain my father's son. I at least can speak my mind concerning the beliefs and opinions which I have inherited from my ancestors, without fearing to snap the bond that unites me to my people. I can even adopt that "scientific heresy which bears the name of Darwin" without any danger to my Judaism.

In a word, I am my own, and my opinions and feelings are my own. I have no reason for concealing or denying them, for deceiving others or myself. And this spiritual freedom—scoff who will!—I would not exchange or barter for all the emancipation in the world.

IV

SERVING GOD

All Jewish duty, in the last analysis, revolves around love of God. In being true to oneself, to society, to one's people, one is being true to God. Thus traditional Jewish literature knows little of the distinctions we have introduced, for purpose of study and analysis, into the concept of Jewish responsibility. A *mitzvah* is a sacred act, man's response to God's will. It is the point of time in which man converts himself and his world to God's service, transforming them both by the will, become deed, directed to God. The Jew, so to speak, does good because he is commanded to. Rabbi Simlai said there were 613 basic commandments; but with elaboration and specification there are, in the fulness of Jewish life, many more.

The climax of all Jewish duty involves the acts immediately and directly related to God Himself, those which provide the continuing sense of God's presence. Knowledge of God for the Jew means knowing himself to be commanded. Drawing close to God is therefore the supreme commandment.

Of all the duties which might be considered in relation to God, there is none to prove the existence of God. In the Jewish view, the existence of God is taken for granted. At the very beginning of Jewish life, as recorded in the Bible, a godless universe was unthinkable after all that had happened to Israel. The Exodus, the covenant at Sinai, the occupation of the Land, all pointed to a power beyond man. Israel saw its faith confirmed in its later history, in the grandeur of nature and the inner experience of man.

In the Middle Ages, when Judaism was confronted by the challenges of Arabic and Christian rationalism, Jewish philosophers attempted to create systematic demonstrations of the existence of God. But this remained a concern of the intellectual élite. For the majority, stress was on what God expected of man rather than on man's speculation about God's essence.

The earliest Jewish approach to the Almighty was to offer sacrifices. The Bible records, however, that there were individuals who did not hesitate to speak to God, who offered words of praise and gratitude, who uttered expressions of trust and confidence. In time, prayer became common and, when the Temple was destroyed in 70 C.E., group liturgy replaced the sacrificial system. Such prayer, though based on individual effort, could not be left to individual whim. As the central means by which the entire people could approach their Father and renew their relationship with Him, structure was needed.

Jews were still encouraged to pray whatever their hearts prompted but a formal liturgy was developed enabling all the members of the house of Israel to pray together for themselves and for the entire people. As the single Jew joined his people in prayer and gained a sense of belonging to the people of Israel, standing together before its God, a new personal and communal Jewish religious experience was born. Communal prayer thus became one of the duties of the Jew.

While other peoples and other religions have taught the need for prayer, Judaism remains unique in holding that study is an equally direct avenue leading toward God. Classic Jewish literature repeats over and over again the need to study as a fundamental religious duty. The ignoramus, as Hillel said, cannot be truly pious. The purpose of learning is not utilitarian—to get a better job or win power. It is not, ideally, to gain honor and respect among Jews.

The purpose of learning is to find out more about God's sacred law and lore. It is to discover the will of God and to learn what men should do in order to live according to that will. The heroes of Jewish culture through the ages have not been warriors or generals—Jews have admired the *talmid hakham,* the "wise student," the man of learning. True, not every Jew can be a scholar, but all those who accept Jewish values do revere the scholar and do seek a little learning of their own—if only that which is a regular part of the morning prayers.

Prayer and study are not the only roads toward religious living. There are also numerous ritual acts to perform, which give a sacred context to the day, the week, the year, the individual life. They provide the Jew with a sense of the holiness of time. Foremost is observance of the Sabbath, the most sacred day in the Jewish calendar, the only one mentioned in the Ten Commandments. It is a day filled with a special ceremonial and permeated by a unique spirit. Its message of rest and release, of cessation from labor, of the needs of the spirit, has special significance in our hectic era.

Finally and climactically, all these duties culminate in love of God. Judaism understands that some people may worship God and fulfill His commandments because they fear His power and His might.

Yet, the Rabbis reiterated what the Bible had said, that God is best served out of love. That is why, to this day, the proclamation "Hear O Israel" in Jewish worship is immediately succeeded, by rabbinic decree, by the Biblical paragraph which begins, "And thou shalt love the Lord, thy God, with all thy heart, with all thy soul, and with all thy might . . ." Love of God is the *first* duty of the man who proclaims God One, and the *last.*

9

Prayer

Prayer is the most immediately identifiable religious act to modern men. Perhaps that is why it is such a problem for them. Insofar as they consider themselves religious they know they should participate in worship. Yet modern men pray less regularly than did their fathers and, while it cannot be measured, they seem to be less involved in the service when they do take part.

In the Jewish community that general problem is complicated by many others: the place of Hebrew in the service, the retention or revision of the centuries-old structure of the service, the sociology of flight from Judaism and return in the suburban synagogue. Many efforts have been made to make the service more appealing to the worshippers: tasteful buildings, music, modern translations, thoughtful readings, creative services, new prayerbooks. While each has attracted adherents, none has come close to meeting the problem.

Is there something in the act of praying itself which puts off modern men? They do not like public displays of emotion or take easily to expressing their feelings. How then can they find ease and pleasure in prayer which is meaningless if it does not come from the full heart? They spend their days calculating and manipulating, striving to gain advantage and get ahead. Prayer is not a contest but honest communication. If one tries to use it to win a concession from God, no matter how cleverly, it is blasphemy. God is not to be wheedled or outwitted in prayer: He is to be spoken to. How then can man pray today when the art of simple, non-exploitive conversation is dead among us?

More difficult is the fact that prayer involves God as well as man. If our society warps men so that they themselves are incompetent to pray, what does it do to their belief in God? They are pressured to cynicism where they might prefer sincerity, to skepticism where they might humbly believe.

Thus, when men come to pray, they are filled with doubts and questions. Before they can utter a phrase from their Prayerbook a dozen qualifications cross their minds. If it is praise, they wonder why God needs it. If it is petition, they worry whether God can do anything about it. If it is thanksgiving, they reflect on how much they themselves had to do to make possible their blessings. What should be communication becomes reflection. What is meant to be dialogue flounders in self-analysis.

Even if we can learn the art of being true to ourselves and what we believe, if we can transcend our sophistication enough to pray, we are beset by the distance between our individual concerns and the Jewish Prayerbook's required prayers. We confuse the poetry of the utterance with statements of fact or description, in part because everything is printed as if it were prose, in part because the old Biblical and rabbinic images are unfamiliar to us. We are put off by ancient memories and group concerns which are alien to us now. The gap between our private selves and our Jewish loyalties, between ourselves as universal men and members of the Jewish people, is rarely more evident.

Some of these questions are new to Judaism. Others are very old, as is implied in the following selection from *Hovot ha-Levavot* (*The Duties of Hearts*). This work was written by Bahya ibn Pakuda, who lived in Spain during the first half of the eleventh century. Little is known of Bahya except that he was a philosopher and a *dayyan* (judge of a Jewish court). His book, the first systematic effort to discuss the major ethical and spiritual motifs of Judaism apart from the practices which regulated them, was written because Bahya found many Jews paying attention only to the outward observance of the law but ignoring its ideas and sentiments. He therefore stressed the importance of doing religious duties with joyful readiness.

Hovot ha-Levavot was widely read and highly regarded by medieval Jewry. Philosophers esteemed its discussion of man's nature, mystics benefitted from its concern for inner purity, and common men found in it an understanding guide to a more richly human existence. When printing came into wide use the ongoing value of Bahya's work was quickly evidenced by the numerous editions which were published. Its continuing utilization by students of Judaism entitles it to be considered one of the great classics of Jewish ethical literature.

FROM

The Duties of Hearts

(Eighth Treatise, Chapter III)

BY BAHYA IBN PAKUDA

A person should examine his religious activities carefully and be as zealous in fulfilling them as he would be in serving a human sovereign. When a king imposes a task calling for physical exertion upon one of his subjects, that subject will not spare himself. He will direct his efforts and abilities toward accomplishing the task. If it is one that calls for deep study and reflection, he will concentrate upon it with all his mental faculties carefully and zealously. If he has to thank his king for a favor conferred upon him or for some kindness shown him, in writing or orally, in verse or in prose, he will not neglect to employ a fine literary style, rhetorical forms, metaphors, figures of speech, hyperbole, true words and perhaps false ones.

There is nothing that one would say about the king that would not be carefully thought out and set forth. If one could demonstrate his devotion to his king with all his limbs, with his inner as well as his outer being, he would do so. If he could move heaven and earth and all that is in them by his praise and gratitude, he would do so. He would do all this for his monarch despite the weakness and insignificance of human beings and their mortality.

The intelligent person engaged in any activity pertaining to the service of God should behave similarly. Such an activity belongs to one of three classes:

The first class consists of activities that are exclusively subjective, what we shall call "duties of the heart" (the exposition of which is our aim in this book).

The second class consists of duties that require movement and are, at the same time, in a composite sense duties of the heart—such as recital of prayers, study of Torah, praise and laudation of God, study of secular subjects, promotion of goodness, and warning against evil.

The third class consists of duties that require only physical activities and in which the heart has no part except the feeling of devotion to God as they are undertaken. Such active duties are the laws regarding dwelling in the *sukkah,* taking the *lulav* and other plants in hand on the Festival of Tabernacles, putting fringes on the corners of garments, affixing the *mezuzah,** observing the Sabbath and Festivals, giving charity. In these and similar duties, one does not need to concentrate on their intent while performing them but the fulfillment of the precept alone suffices.

However, when duties of the heart are to be fulfilled, a person must clear his mind of all worldly thoughts and cares and devote his heart and inward being to God alone during the time he is engaged in their performance. It is related of one of the ancient ascetics that, while he was reciting his prayers, he was wont to exclaim: "My God! My grief at not fulfilling my duty to You has annulled all my other griefs and my anxiety over this failure has removed all my other anxieties." For this, God accepted his pious service and was pleased with him. That is what our sages meant when they said: "Religious duties require concentration."

If one is engaged in a composite duty of the heart, one that also calls for physical movement (such as saying a prayer), he should disengage his body from other activities and free his mind from all thoughts that would distract him. After washing off any dirt

* The small case, affixed to the entry of the Jewish home, in which are contained a parchment with the first two paragraphs of the liturgical version of the *Shema,* "Hear O Israel." They refer to the commandment "to write them upon the doorposts of thy house . . ."

and moving away from anything objectionable, he should then consider in his heart to whom he intends to offer his prayer, what he seeks therein, and the words and terms with which he should address his Maker.

We know that words merely uttered with the tongue are like a shell, while meditation on the words is in the heart and is the kernel. Words are the body of prayer; meditation on their meaning is the spirit. If one prays with his tongue and his heart is otherwise engaged, his prayer is like a body without a spirit, or a shell without a kernel, because only the body is present while the heart is absent.

Of such a person Scripture says: *This people draw near, And with their mouth and with their lips do honor Me, but they have removed their heart far from Me.* Such a person may be compared to a servant who, when his master returned home, bade his wife and the members of his family to show honor to the master and provide him with every service. He, however, neither busied himself to show his master honor nor did aught that would have befitted him. His master was so angry with him that he refused them all with contempt.

Thus too, if a person is saying prayers and his heart is empty, not concentrating on the contents of the prayer, the Almighty will not accept his prayer which was only mechanical, a mere movement of the tongue. *Let the words of my mouth and the meditation of my heart be acceptable to You.* If a person, while praying, thinks of a worldly matter, whether permitted or forbidden, and then, concluding his prayer, says: *May the meditation of my heart be acceptable to You,* would it not be highly disgraceful for him to claim that he had communed with God in his heart and mind, and then petition the Almighty to accept that prayer and be pleased with its recital by him? Such a person is like one of whom it is said: *Yet they seek Me daily and delight to know My ways as if they were a nation that did righteousness.*

Our wise men say: "A man should judge for himself: if he feels that he can pray devoutly, let him say the prayers. If he cannot do so, let him not say them." In the same sense, Rabbi Eleazar included in his parting admonitions to his disciples the exhortation: "When you pray, be conscious before whom you stand." Scripture also says: *Prepare to meet your God, O Israel.*

Our sages say: "And when you pray, do not let your prayer be fixed and routine but make it an appeal for mercy and a personal supplication to the Almighty." Scripture says: *When my soul was humbled within me, I remembered the Lord and I directed my prayer unto You in Your holy Temple;* further: *Let us lift up our hearts with our hands unto God in the heavens.*

It is proper, brother, for you to know that our devotion in prayer is nothing but the soul's longing for God, humbling itself in His presence, exalting its Creator, offering praises and thanksgiving to His Name, casting all its burdens upon Him. Since it is difficult for the soul to recall all this without orderly composition and arrangement, our teachers wrote prayers concerning those things which most classes of people need, and in which their lack and dependence upon God are most evident.

These constitute the *siddur t'fillotenu,* the Order of our Prayers, properly arranged and set forth, wherewith the soul can worthily greet its Creator without being ashamed when it prostrates itself before Him. In reciting these well-ordered prayers with a devout heart, the soul's appropriate humility and lowliness before God are manifested.

Then too, because thought changes rapidly and is unstable, owing to the swiftness with which fancies pass through the mind, and it is therefore difficult for every individual to arrange the subjects of prayer for himself, our sages put them in suitable terms for the individual to repeat in proper order. They did this because they knew that the soul's thoughts follow their expression and they are drawn forth by man's words.

Prayer consists of words and their meanings. Words need an idea but ideas do not need verbalization if they can be put in orderly fashion in the heart. Since the participation of the heart is the essence of our devotion and the chief aim to which our attention should be directed, therefore, my brother, arrange the contents of your prayer in proper form in your heart. Let it correspond with the words which you are about to utter. Let your words and your thoughts be directed to God.

Keep your body free from unnecessary movements. Restrain your senses and your imagination during your prayers, so that they do not wander off to secular matters. Let your behavior be as wholehearted as it would be if you were standing in the presence of your king, praising and lauding him and recounting his good deeds, even though he would be ignorant of what is in your heart. How much more should such be your behavior toward the exalted Creator who contemplates your external and inward being, who sees what is visible in your life and what is concealed.

Your recital of prayers is a mark of the Creator's faith in you, for He has placed it fully under your control while none besides Him contemplates it. If you pray as He bids you, you will have discharged the obligation imposed by His faith in you and He will accept this service from you.

But, if you are not faithful with your heart and with your tongue, you belong to the class of those who rob Him of His faith in you, and of such people Scripture says: *For they are a treacherous breed, children with no loyalty in them.*

On the other hand, even concerning people of different faiths who conduct themselves in accordance with their laws and rules, Scripture says: *Mine eyes are upon the faithful of the land that they may dwell with Me.*

If one is fulfilling an active duty, such as erecting a booth and dwelling therein during the Festival of Tabernacles, or taking the representative plant species on the same festival, or carrying out any of the other precepts we have mentioned as belonging to this third class of commandments, he should first direct his heart to God before He performs the precept; the root of his act should be the sentiment of obedience to the Creator's commandments, the wish to magnify and exalt Him, to thank and praise Him for His great benefits and abundant lovingkindnesses.

Thus he will attain the ultimate purpose of this service at its beginning, during its performance, and at its completion. For the goal of these commandments is to fear God, to do what will please Him and to keep from anything that would anger Him. As David said: *O my God, I delight to do Your will.*

In all these active duties one should observe a procedure similar to what I mentioned at the beginning of this section as the conduct proper in the presence of a king, and should ever keep it in mind. And so, with God's help, he will feel in his limbs zest in fulfillment of the service, as is expressed in the words of David which we have previously quoted: *I thought on my ways, and turned my feet unto Your testimonies. I made haste and delayed not, to keep Your commandments.*

10

Study

The inadequacy of the present-day Jewish community is most disturbingly visible in its unprecedented ignorance of Judaism and things Jewish. Nor is there reason to believe that this situation will soon change. We live in a society which respects business success and social status, which thinks consumption an art and art an industry, which considers the search for new forms of entertainment an important use of time.

In the larger society, education remains essentially a means to a more important end. High school students are warned of unemployment without a diploma and the lifetime virtues of a college degree have been reckoned to the nearest thousand dollars of income. Though adult education is on the rise, people are striving mainly to get new jobs or embellish their expertise in the midst of an information explosion. Even our recreational education is for the sake of accomplishment, to win ribbons, money or new friends.

Study for study's sake seems appropriate only for some academics and eccentrics. Study as a religious exercise, as a means of being more fully a man knowledgeable in the word of God, is relatively unknown. Yet that is the Jewish ideal and, in the past, the experience of many Jews. Jews today tend to devote their energies to making a living and mastering the affluent way of life. Though many Jews succeed to an incredible extent in secular scholarship and research, they are often satisfied to remain children in their knowledge of Judaism.

Obviously, the past cannot always supply answers to new problems. But it can present us with standards and ideals. At least we can learn what the student used to mean in Jewish life and how Jews felt about those who dedicated themselves to

Torah. We can learn something of the passion for study which undoubtedly underlies the current concern among Jews for secular education. Perhaps, too, we can find a way to translate this image from another culture style into one appropriate to our own.

One of the best pictures of the East European Jewish scholarly ideal is to be found in Haim Nahman Bialik's poem, *Ha-Matmid.* Bialik (1873–1934) ranks as the leading Hebrew poet since the Golden Age in Spain.

Born in Russia, Bialik grew up in the intensive Jewish environment of the *shtetl.* He lived through the close of one epoch of Jewish history, the end of the East European community, and the beginning of a new one, the era of immigration and the rebuilding of Zion. He expressed the tangled emotions and difficult experiences of a people in transition. He became the voice of a generation of Jews that despised the bitter, ugly life of exile and oppression and awoke to the possibilities of a wholesome life in the renewed homeland. Bialik, in a word, was *the* national poet, the lyric interpreter of his people's renaissance, exerting a profound influence on his own generation and those that followed.

One of Bialik's early masterpieces was *Ha-Matmid,* translated freely as "The Talmud Student" or "The Perpetual Student." The Hebrew conveys much more: *matmid* derives from the root used for the daily sacrifice; it denotes a scholar so desirous of learning that he willingly sacrifices food, sleep, wealth, all physical and material pleasures for study. The *matmid* was literally a perpetual student, someone who could not bear to put aside the sacred books even briefly. Though Bialik was fully aware that the ideal was passing, he recognized that the *matmid* and the House of Study constituted the secret of Jewish endurance and a powerhouse of Jewish creativity.

Ha-Matmid pictures an age that no longer exists. Jewish intellectuals in great numbers now pursue secular academic careers, but seldom study the Jewish classics. The day of the *matmid* is as good as gone, but is a modern equivalent possible?

The Talmud Student

(Selected Stanzas)

BY HAIM NAHMAN BIALIK

There are abandoned corners of our Exile,
Remote, forgotten cities of dispersion,
Where still in secret burns our ancient light,
Where God has saved a remnant from disaster.
There, brands that glimmer in a ruin of ashes,
Pent and unhappy souls maintain the vigil—
Spirits grown old beyond the count of time,
Grown old beyond the reckoning of days.
And when thou goest forth alone, at nightfall,
Wandering in one of these, the sacred cities,
When heaven above is quick with breaking stars,
And earth beneath with whispering spirit-winds—
Thine ear will catch the murmur of a voice,
Thine eye will catch the twinkle of a light
Set in a window, and a human form—
A shadow trembling, swaying back and forth,
A voice, an agony, that lifts and falls,
And comes toward thee upon the waves of silence.
Mark well the swaying shadow and the voice:
It is a *matmid* in his prison-house,
A prisoner, self-guarded, self-condemned,
Self-sacrificed to study of the law.
Within these walls, within this prison-house,
Six years have passed above his swaying form:
Within these walls the child became the youth,
The youth became the man, fore-ripened swift;
And swift as these went, swifter yet were gone
The cheek's bloom and the lustre of his eyes.

Six years have passed since first he set his face
To the dark corner of the inner walls;
Six years since he has seen, for joyous sunlight,
Gray limestone, lizards and the webs of spiders;
Six years of hunger, years of sleeplessness,
Six years of wasting flesh and falling cheeks—
He knows that Jews have studied thus of old,
He knows the fame and glory they have won . . .

Yet even in this mournful swamp the days
Bring change, and hope of change—but not for him:
Others less condemned, whose sentences
Admit of commutation, boys whose hearts
Thrill to the call of freedom from afar:
Twice in the twelve-month revolution comes,
The impatient spirits from their bondage break,
The gray walls of the prison are abandoned.
Some will come back, some are forever free;
Familiar faces pass, strange ones return.
Some to the neighboring villages escape,
Far from the overseer's relentless eye,
And there begin new lives of ease and honor
Under the shelter of some good man's roof
Proud of a scholarly adoptive son;
And some are driven out in dark dishonor
And homeward tread the crooked path of shame—
One for the nights he gave to playing cards,
Another for the nights he gave to wenches;
A third, impatient of the Sabbath law,
Chose a queer place in which to smoke his pipe;
A fourth was studious—in forbidden books;
And still another—for unpublished crimes.
And sometimes one is chosen for a husband
And weds a plump and solid village girl;
Another, pure of name, becomes a rabbi
And finds a place of honor in the city.
But one stays nailed and rooted in his place,

For him no change or revolution comes—
The phantoms of the years behind him pass,
The iron wall, unchanging, stands in front . . .

Oi, Oi, amar Raba, amar Abbaye,
*Thus Raba said and thus Abbaye taught.**

(Backward and forward swaying he repeats
With ceaseless sing-song the undying words.)
Is this the smithy, then; is this the anvil
Where a people's soul is forged? Is this the source
From which the life-blood of a people flows,
To feed the generations yet unborn,
And knit the muscles of heroes yet to come?
What voices, then, are these that ring, what flames
On which the heart mounts to the topmost heavens?
Who filled these pages with undying magic?
Whence comes the power that makes these mildewed words
Light flames of passion in a heart outlived,
Strike living sparks in eyes that are extinguished . . .

"*Oi amar Raba* . . . it may come to pass—
Who knows? Who knows? My soul may yet be taken
A sacrifice, as I have offered it,
Upon the altar of God: and from this corner
My glory may arise to fill the world. . .
Oi, tanu rabbanan . . . till forty years
The great Akiba was an empty vessel,
A shepherd ignorant, and he became,
Through study of the Torah, like a banner
Unto his people . . . and I am yet a boy.
O God, I pray Thee, take me as I ask,
Take all Thou wilt, my body and its blood,
For I am vowed to Thee and to Thy Torah.
For her my lips will move, for her my voice
Will never fail, and for her sake I stand
Firm rooted to my place and move not hence:

* These phrases introduce many of the discussions of the Talmud.

For her my body knows no rest, for her
These eyes shall ask in vain for sleep, until
The thirst that burns my soul is satisfied.
With earliest dawn I will awake, keep vigil
Through half the night till I have conquered all,
Till I am master of the sacred lore.
And therefore—*Amar Raba* . . ." Once again
The voice takes strength and rings across the air.
It seemed to me that there, above the Ark,
A subtle light was lit, as of a smile—
God's smile of tenderness above his child,
Or, who can tell, a smile of mockery
For those who, yet alive, have found their graves,
Delivering up their souls unto the Torah . . .

And days come even when that heart, rebelling,
Knows its own bitterness and wilts with pain.
The winter brings the time of ice and storm;
The skies are ashen, earth is desolate,
The fierce rain downward slants, the sullen rock
Drags wearily across the stifled skies.
Oh, for a single glimpse of sunlight then,
One tiny fleeting gift of light and warmth.
There comes instead a spider from its den
To pitch its green-gray tent above the boy.
Deep darkness fills his corner and his heart,
A shivering cold pervades his spirit's chambers.
Then the boy knows that he has been forgotten;
A trembling falls upon him; lost! forgotten!
Abandoned utterly unto the darkness!
And fear comes that the strength which has endured
Will fail, and the eternal flame be quenched.
And then his voice ascends as from a man
Who dying lies, and knows that he must die,
And chants the lamentation for himself;
Then all the learning of the boy is changed
Into a mourning song, wherein are mingled

Despair and bitterness and consolation.
Are these the moments of thy bitterness,
Welcomed with love, part of thy sacrifice?
Knowest thou, unhappy one, thou art unhappy?

Unhappy? Wherefore? Who shall demonstrate
That the wide world is each man's heritage?
Let him rejoice, perhaps, even for the corner
God granted him that he might stand therein.
The mighty Torah, the immortal light,
Has always sought dark corners for itself.
From the wombs of darkness to the light of day,
Successive generations bring her forth
A heritage beneath the hand of God.
Like thieves in attics and cellars gathered
Our sons have studied the forbidden Torah,
And glorious inextinguishably bright
Have issued from these cellars, while from attics
A people's saints and leaders have come down.
Dear to the Torah is the life of sorrow,
And in the chastity of poverty
The people and its sons have kept the faith.
Why should he take it ill, then, that the world
And all its treasures must be locked from him?
See! he has locked within his heart, forever,
Two of the ponderous tractates; can repeat
Each page, each column, and each syllable.
His fellow students eye him enviously—
Foresee his triumph in days to come.
Two tractates whole! How happy is his lot!
Shall not the inward heart of him rejoice
Who plucks so soon the payment of his toil?
Two titles has he—wonder child and scholar.*
One jewel shines upon the High Priest's brow,

* A child prodigy in Eastern Europe was referred to as an *iluey,* an outstanding one, a "wonder child." The truly learned scholar who had mastered the many classic texts was called a *talmid hakham,* literally "a wise student" but meaning more—a master of knowledge.

One crown of laurel is the poet's prize,
One wreath of bays is to the hero given;
One for the wonder-child, one for the scholar.
On the sky-soaring ladder of the Torah,
It's only one step more to rank of *Gaon*.
Have many reached the glory which is his? . . .
Who cast the bitter note that rings
In the dark Talmud-melody, a sound
That clutches at the heart and sunders it?
He only who in midnight's silent hour
Or in the quiet dusk before the dawn,
The old *yeshivah* passes, stands a while
And through the window hears the lonely voice
Pouring sweet bitterness and bitter sweetness
Upon the whispering breeze—'tis he alone
Can know the burning anguish of the chant,
The pain, the pathos of the Talmud-song . . .

I, in my boyhood, was a listener
Among the voices, and my youth was passed
With these wan sufferers, whose wrinkled brows
And staring eyes implore the world's compassion.
And every wrinkle spoke to me in silence
Of passions stifled and of fires extinguished,
And for each wrinkle of their pallid faces
My heart was torn as with a searing flame . . .
And now when in my memory rise those voices,
Those dying lamentations in the night,
The heart in me cries out: Lord of the world!
To what end is this mighty sacrifice?

My fate denied I should be lost with you
Unhappy ones! and to the hearth you knew
Long, long ago I said farewell forever.
My Torah is abandoned: for the sake of bread
I have known sin; and though I too am lost,
It was a lonely road of mine own choosing.
The times have changed; far from your boundaries

In alien places have I raised my altar.
All, all of you do I remember yet,
In all my wanderings you go with me,
Your likeness graven in my heart forever.
And I remember, too, how strong, how sturdy
The seed must be that withers in those fields,
How rich would be the blessing if one beam
Of living sunlight could break through to you;
How great the harvest to be reaped in joy,
If once the wind of life should pass through you,
And blow clear through to the *yeshivah* doors . . .
All, all of you do I remember yet—
The hungry childhood and the bitter manhood,
And my heart weeps for my unhappy people . . .
How burned, how blasted must our portion be,
If seed like this is withered in its soil . . .

11

Observing the Sabbath

Of all Jewish religious observances, none is more sacred than the Sabbath. The Rabbis considered it a foretaste of life in the world-to-come. Through long centuries of toil and oppression, the Sabbath was regarded as a special gift from God to the children of Israel. Sholom Aleichem has Tevyeh say: "Why does a man work the whole week long? You work a whole week to reach the Sabbath . . . naturally. I tell you, a man wouldn't know what to do if God hadn't given us the Sabbath. A gift—a real gift out of His grace. When the Sabbath comes, I'm a different man."

Bialik, who was finely attuned to the soul of the Jewish tradition, once wrote in a letter: "The Sabbath is the greatest creation of the Hebrew spirit and whoever deprecates it deprecates the very essence of Judaism."

In our day, Sabbath observance presents a complex problem, mainly because of the rapid pace at which everyone is expected to live. This very fact could well make the Sabbath a welcome break in the hectic routine, a reminder that we are not the slaves of clock and phone and calendar. But much of our leisure hours are filled with recreational activities which we often invest with the same anxious concern as we do our regular days. Even vacations tend to be more exhausting than regenerative. Modern man seems helpless in the face of the tempo of life he has created.

Even for those who wish to observe the Sabbath, life in a predominantly non-Jewish atmosphere poses difficulties. What then are we to do? Is it better to recite the *kiddush* and to have a Sabbath atmosphere on Friday evening even if one goes to work on Saturday, or is it more honest, if one cannot follow the full traditional pattern, to do nothing at all about Sabbath observance?

A sixteenth century mystic named Haim Vital gave spiritual guidance on this very question to Jews of his generation in a work called *Hok Leyisrael.* Vital lived in the city of Safed in Palestine, an important mystical center in that period following the expulsion from Spain. *Hok Leyisrael* was very popular in the centuries following its publication, perhaps because mysticism became one of the chief consolations of the desolate, downtrodden Jewish people.

Vital discusses the mystical significance of the Sabbath, emphasizing one's inner preparation and a literal acceptance of the Talmudic references to angelic visitors and extra souls which come on the Sabbath. These private religious experiences are linked with the practices which Judaism prescribes, a blending typical of Jewish mysticism. Indeed, Vital, assuming that the reader knows all the Sabbath laws, confines his instructions to the attitudes one should bring to their practice.

Vital stresses the need to prepare properly for the Sabbath so that it may be a day of true physical and spiritual delight. His advice to wear one's best clothes and to serve delicacies remains pertinent as does his counsel to the family to recite the *kiddush,* to the father to bless his children, and to husband and wife to refrain from quarreling.

FROM

Hok Leyisrael

(*Appended Musar section*)

BY HAIM VITAL

1. The Rabbis have said that anyone who wishes to appear before a king must be properly dressed, pointing to the statement that one should not come unto the king dressed in sackcloth. Whoever plans to appear before royalty usually spends a full day decking himself out in finery. This is what the sages meant when they stated: "Prepare yourself in the antechamber before you

enter the palace." In the same way, one must get ready for the Sabbath and prepare oneself to greet the King properly, with dignity and joy.

2. Thus, one has to prepare oneself to receive the heavenly visitors that come down to spend the Sabbath with Israel. By changing the vowels of one Hebrew word in the command to observe the Sabbath, we understand that this is so: in the phrase, "to keep the Sabbath unto all generations," the Hebrew word for "unto all generations" or "unto *their* generations," *ledoratam,* can be read *ladur ittam,* which means "to dwell with them."

Therefore, everyone must prepare a fitting abode for the Divine Presence and the heavenly guests. This abode is in one's heart and it should contain beautiful objects and fine furniture, that is one's limbs. There are three things which intensify one's consciousness: a beautiful inner dwelling, beautiful furniture for it, and a beautiful wife. The beautiful wife is the soul wherein the Divine Presence rests.

The additional souls are called guests. Whoever is worthy meets these blessed guests with the joy of the *Shabbat* and will find that his soul will later be met, in the world-to-come, with equal joy and delight. Similarly, human guests should be welcomed on the *Shabbat* with much joy and delight.

3. When one buys something for the Sabbath, he should keep in mind that he is doing so to honor the *Shabbat.* It is said that the perspiration resulting from a person's labors in behalf of the Sabbath is the erasing fluid with which God wipes away man's sins. Therefore, let every person exert himself greatly in honor of the *Shabbat.* He should not worry lest he demean himself in so doing, for whatever he does to honor the Sabbath truly adds to his own honor.

4. One should prepare beautiful garments and set them aside for the Sabbath. The honor of the *Shabbat* is discerned in one's garments since they are worn at the inception of the Sabbath. One of the mystics has stated that whoever wears garments of splendor on the Sabbath will wear such garments in the world-to-come. At the time when a person removes his weekday clothes, let him also remove his sins and repent. When he dons his Sab-

bath garb, he should think about drawing on extra holiness, about devoting himself to virtue and good conduct.

It is not enough, however, merely to have such intentions. One must indeed cast off all evil. As long as one remains defiled in his heart, no Sabbath preparations will help and one will remain estranged from holiness. Therefore, when a person commits himself to the Sabbath and to goodness, he should do so with all sincerity; he will then find that heaven will help him to achieve his purpose.

Women should also put on fine clothes, before they light the candles. If one is so poor that she has no special Sabbath dress, she should at least cover herself with a white sheet. If she notices that the time for kindling the candles has arrived and she has not yet put on her Sabbath dress, she should light the candles first and change her clothes afterwards.

It should be pointed out that, even though she may be able to afford to do so, a woman should not dress ostentatiously. She should not deck herself out in jewelry as this arouses jealousy among non-Jews; much trouble has resulted from such actions.

5. (One must pray at sundown before eating the evening Sabbath meal.) After services, a man should go directly home without dawdling so that his family will not tire and fall asleep waiting for him, thereby missing the *kiddush* or the Sabbath meal.

6. All Jews should bless their sons and daughters on the Sabbath eve. They do this by placing both hands on their heads and saying: "May the Lord make you like Ephraim and Menasseh," Joseph's prosperous sons. He should also add the priestly blessing. In addition, one may add whatever is in one's heart. . . . Since parents may lose their tempers during the week and say that which they do not really mean, one invokes blessings at the time of the Sabbath joy to counteract these words.

7. Our sages urge harmony on the Sabbath between one man and another and between husband and wife. Of this it is said: "You shall honor Him," which means that you should honor the Sabbath by not quarreling.

8. One is not permitted to be sad on the Sabbath. We have seen

people with good cause for pain dispel it by their acceptance of the Sabbath joy.

9. The holy Sabbath protects us in exile. It is our shield. When Israel did not respect the Sabbath properly, enemies attacked her. If it were not for the *Shabbat,* we would have disappeared from the face of the earth.

10. Food and drink on Sabbath and holy days should not be intended just to satisfy the body. Food and drink should be enjoyed in order that the soul may delight. Stimulating the powers of the body should serve to strengthen the powers of the soul.

11. The eve of the Sabbath is a proper time to repent one's wrongdoings. One should turn away from all wrong acts done during the week. Therefore, one ought to examine his deeds before the Sabbath and correct what needs correction. This should be done in order not to enter upon the Sabbath in defilement.

12. The Biblical command to observe the Sabbath reads *"ledoratam,"* which, as has been noted above in paragraph 2, means that the Sabbath comes to dwell with the Jews. This teaches that, with the advent of the Sabbath, a messenger from on high comes to observe whether the Jew has properly cleaned and prepared his home, table, bed and lights. If the home is found to be as it should be, the messenger says: "This is truly a Jewish home!" If not, the messenger says: "This is not a Jewish home!"

13. When a Jew keeps the holy Sabbath as prescribed by Jewish law, he can sense the additional soul that he acquires for the day. Both body and soul delight thereon, for Sabbath joy is one-sixtieth of that of the world-to-come.

14. The three days preceding a Sabbath and the three days following it are sustained by the holy day. The Sabbath is the heart of the week, pulsating life into all other parts of the body. Delight in the Sabbath and your heart will be delighted, measure for measure.

12

Loving God

To speak of love of God is strange to modern man. We are not even certain we believe in God; love of Him seems sentimental and saccharine. What can love of God really mean?

It means that it is not enough to think about God. While concepts of marriage and analyses of family life may be very useful, they are no substitute for the experience of getting married and living in a family. Similarly, loving God means bringing to our religion our hearts, our very selves. If faith does not involve us at the very core of our being, if it does not touch us at the place where we live, it is not true faith.

Love also involves responsibility. If our relationship is a real one, there are things our beloved expects of us, words to be said, dates to be remembered, services to render, a presence to cultivate. There are things we may not do lest we violate the trust placed in us or show ourselves unworthy of the love given us. Because we have been so graced, we cannot be satisfied with what we have been but must become truer and more deserving of our love. Our problem in loving God is less His distance than the human inability truly to love man. Using each other as we do, hiding from the reality of what one person might mean to another, how can we aspire to love of God?

Moreover, love is not a function of clear and distinct knowledge. We need not understand all about our sweethearts to pledge ourselves to them for life. Must we then know with precision what we mean by "God"? Is it necessary or even conceivable for us to define Him? In the past, Jews were satisfied less with knowing what God was and more with understanding His demands of men. One of the Hasidic masters, Rabbi Levi Yitzhak of Berditchev, put it this way: "I do not ask You, Lord of the world, to reveal to me the secrets of Your ways—I could not comprehend them. And I do not ask to know *why* I suffer, but only this: do I suffer for Your sake?"

Mordecai M. Kaplan and other modern thinkers have attempted to define clearly what they mean by God. Some, like Martin Buber, however, have insisted that it is futile to search for definitions. What is needed rather is to turn in openness to Him even as a man turns to his neighbor in friendship. Both schools have felt He may be found, though they have sought Him in differing ways. And both have felt that in man's search for God's presence he gives his existence purpose and direction.

Such was the view of R. Moshe Haim Luzzatto (1707–1747), an Italian mystic who wrote Hebrew poetry and plays, and is regarded by some as the initiator of modern Hebrew literature.

Luzzatto was sufficiently of the older world to believe that heavenly voices spoke to him, revealing unknown mysteries. There are even those who think that he regarded himself in a Messianic light; indeed, the Italian rabbinate found his influence unhealthy and forbade him to teach his mystical doctrines. For a while, Luzzatto accepted their decrees. But too overwhelmed by his mystic insights to keep them to himself, he soon resumed his teaching; he was placed under the ban and his writings were condemned.

Luzzatto decided to leave Italy for the freer atmosphere of Holland. After several years in Amsterdam, Luzzatto settled in the Holy Land. He died in 1747 at the age of forty.

It was while living on Dutch soil that Luzzatto composed *Mesillat Yesharim* (*The Path of the Upright*). This book is an ethical work that seeks to show the way to attain true piety and saintliness. Its aim is religious perfection, its premise that moral conduct requires training in order to overcome the many obstacles continually threatening it. The author outlines a practical course of moral and religious self-discipline for the thoughtful layman. Luzzatto's book was widely read in far-flung Jewish communities and in the nineteenth century became a favorite text of the growing Orthodox *Musar* or Ethical Movement.

Luzzatto wrote in the style of his day, liberally quoting Biblical verses that were no doubt familiar to his contemporaries. He assumes that his reader is already devoted to the goal of coming to love God; hence he attempts neither to define nor motivate. He merely outlines what he thinks love of God means.

FROM

The Path of the Upright

(*Chapter 19*)

BY MOSES HAIM LUZZATTO

We will now treat of the love of God and its three major aspects: joy, devotion, and zeal.

The love of God means fervently wanting to be near Him and pursuing His holiness, just as we pursue whatever we fervently desire. Therefore, mentioning His Name, talking about His wonderful deeds, studying His Torah, and meditating on His divine nature—all of these are a source of pleasure as real as the intense love of a husband for the wife of his youth or of a father for an only son. That is what Jeremiah meant when he said: *For as often as I speak of Him, I do earnestly remember Him.*

It should be obvious that anyone who truly loves his Creator will not neglect worshipping Him, unless he is physically prevented from doing so. He will not wait to be urged or preached at, but he will be prompted by his own heart to worship God and he will do so unless some insurmountable obstacle prevents him.

Such was the practice of the pious in ancient days. As King David said: *As the hart longs for the water brooks, so my soul longs for You, O God. When shall I come and appear before God?* In another psalm he said: *My soul yearns, yea pines for the courts of the Lord.* And, in still another: *My soul thirsts for You, my flesh longs for You.* King David was moved to these avowals because of the tremendous longing which drew him near to God.

Isaiah expressed himself similarly. He said: *Your name and Your remembrance is the desire of our soul. With my soul have I desired You in the night; yea, with my spirit within me have I sought You earnestly.*

David, too, knew such longing and told of the pleasure and delight he felt in talking about God and His glories: *When I remember You upon my couch and meditate upon You in the night watches; I will delight myself in Your commandments which I have loved;* and *Your commandments are my delight.*

Unquestionably, such love must spring from no ulterior motive. Love of God must not be due to the fact that He bestows welfare, wealth and success; it should be as natural and normal as a son's love for his father. As it says in Deuteronomy: *Is He not your father that has begotten you?*

Indeed, the test of this love is hardship and adversity. Commenting on the commandment: *You shall love the Lord your God with all your soul and with all your might,* our sages of the Talmud said: *"With all your soul"* means even at the cost of your life, and *with all your might* means even at the cost of your possessions." In order that hardship and adversity may not make it difficult for us to love God, we can think of them in two ways. One will appeal to the average person; the other will appeal to the wise and profound mind. The first maintains the rabbinic view: "Whatever heaven does is for the best." This means that sufferings and hardships only appear to be evil but, in reality, are good. For example, a surgeon amputates an injured muscle or limb in order to save the rest of the body and to save the person from death. This may seem cruel but is actually an act of mercy and is meant for the individual's good. The patient does not love the surgeon any the less because of what he has done. On the contrary, he loves him more.

In the same way, if a man realizes that whatever God does to him, whether to his person or to his possessions, is intended for his benefit, then he will not lessen his love for God because of suffering or hardship, even though he may not comprehend how he is benefitted. To the contrary, his love would become even more intense and more fervent.

This kind of reasoning is not needed by those who possess true knowledge. Such people do not concentrate on themselves at all. What they pray for is that the glory of God be extolled and that they may be able to afford Him true joy. The greater the hindrances, the happier are they to prove the firmness of their faith. For example, a general who is famous for his heroism prefers to fight where the battle rages most violently, so that everyone will acknowledge his bravery if he proves himself victorious. Likewise, a lover welcomes every opportunity to prove his devotion and his ardor to his beloved. That is how those who love act!

Now, we shall speak of the above-mentioned three aspects of the love of God: devotion, joy and zeal. In devotion, the heart should so cling to God that it has no other interest or concern. The highest form of this virtue is expressed in clinging devotedly to the Creator at all times and in all hours.

Above all, he who loves his Creator should cling to Him devotedly while praying. This can be illustrated by a story told in the Jerusalem Talmud about a scorpion that stung Rabbi Hanina ben Dosa while he was praying. Rabbi Hanina did not interrupt his prayers but continued until he completed them. His disciples then said to him: "Master, did you not feel the sting?" Rabbi Hanina replied: "I will take an oath that I was so absorbed in my prayers that I did not feel a thing."

The Torah often exhorts us to be devoted to God. It says in Deuteronomy: *To love the Lord your God and to cleave to Him,* as well as: *And to Him shall you cleave.* This implies that a man should be so devoted to God that nothing can separate him from Him. R. Simon ben Lakish said: "The love which God bears Israel is designated by three different terms—devotion, longing and happiness." These terms correspond to the three principal aspects of love and are associated with all matters pertaining to the beloved.

The second aspect is joy. It is one of the essentials of the worship of God. King David sang: *Serve the Lord with gladness, come before His presence with singing. Let the righteous be glad; let them exult before the Lord; yea, let them rejoice with gladness.*

Our sages said: "The Divine Presence rests only upon one who finds a joy in the performance of a *mitzvah.*" R. Aibu, commenting on the verse *Serve the Lord with gladness,* was more specific. He inferred from it: "Whenever you are about to pray, let your heart rejoice that you are about to pray to God who is without peer." Here, indeed, is cause for true rejoicing: being privileged to serve the incomparable Lord and to be occupied with His Torah and His commandments. These are the means to attain perfection and glory. The deeper one's penetration into the innermost recesses of the knowledge of God's greatness, the greater the joy and the more exultation of heart.

The psalmist sang: *Let Israel rejoice in its Maker, let the Children of Zion be joyful in their King.* David, who in a great measure attained this goal, said in Psalms: *Let my musing be sweet unto Him; as for me, I will rejoice in the Lord.* He also said: *My lips shall greatly rejoice when I sing praises unto You; and my soul which You have redeemed.*

David was so overcome by inward joy that his lips moved of their own accord and uttered praises while he was meditating on the glories of God. His soul was in such ecstatic rapture that he could conclude: *And my soul which You have redeemed.*

We find that the Holy One, blessed be He, reproaches Israel for failing to attain that state of mind in their worship, as it says in Deuteronomy: *Because you did not serve the Lord your God with joyfulness and with gladness of heart.*

On the other hand, when David saw that Israel reached this high degree of joy when they brought their free-will offerings for the building of the Temple, he prayed that they might retain it forever. He said: *And now have I seen with joy Your people that are present here offer willingly to You. O Lord, the God of Abraham, of Isaac and of Israel our fathers, keep such purposes and thoughts in the hearts of Your people forever, and direct their hearts to You.*

The third aspect of love is zeal. A man should be zealous for the honor of God. He should hate those who hate Him and strive to humble them in every way possible, so that the worship of God be furthered and His glory enhanced. David said in Psalms: *Do I not hate them, O Lord, that hate You? And do I not strive with those who rise up against You? I hate them with utmost hatred; I count them my enemies.* Elijah said something similar: *I have been very zealous for the Lord God of hosts.*

Our sages denounced the man who was able to protest against wrong but did not. They held him responsible for the sin of the wrongdoers. Commenting on the verse from Lamentations: *Her princes are become like harts that find no pasture,* the Rabbis said: "As the harts hide their heads under one another in time of drought, so the great men of Israel turned their faces away from a misdeed in order not to see it. The Holy One, blessed be He, therefore said of them: *The time will come when I will also hide My face from them.*

It is self-evident that, as he who loves his neighbor cannot bear to see him maltreated or insulted, whoever loves the Holy One, blessed be He, cannot bear to see His Name profaned or His commandment desecrated. On the other hand, whoever keeps the Torah and exerts every effort to maintain it cannot restrain himself and be silent. The Holy One, blessed be He, said to Job: *Let loose your furious wrath; glance at every proud one and abase him; tread down the wicked where they stand.* Thus, the love of one who truly loves his Creator is indeed strong. As the psalmist said: *O you who love the Lord, hate evil.*

FURTHER READING

Part I. BEING A DECENT PERSON

Chapter 1. Developing Character

For additional ethical wills, see *Hebrew Ethical Wills,* 2 volumes, compiled and translated by I. Abrahams (Jewish Publication Society, 1928–32), especially Rabbi Eliezer the Great's "The Paths of Life" (Vol. I) and "The Testament of Solomon son of Isaac" and "Letter of Elijah of Vilna" (Vol. II).

For Talmudic views on what constitutes the decent man, see Abraham Cohen, *Everyman's Talmud* (Dutton, 1949), Chapter 7; and C. G. Montefiore and H. Loewe, *A Rabbinic Anthology* (Meridian Paperback, 1960), Chapters 16, 18, 19 and 20.

Chapter 2. Going Beyond the Law

For English translations of Hasidic tales, see Martin Buber, *Tales of the Hasidim,* 2 volumes (Schocken, 1947–8, cloth and paper); see also Buber's *The Legend of the Baal-Shem* (Harper, 1955) and *The Origin and Meaning of Hasidism* (Horizon Press, 1960).

For the role of law in Jewish life in Eastern Europe, see Mark Zborowski and Elizabeth Herzog, *Life Is with People* (International Universities, 1952), particularly "Charity Saves from Death."

For discussion of *halakhah,* see Abraham J. Heschel, *God in Search of Man* (Meridian Paperback, 1961), Chapters 31–34. For relation of ethics to belief in God, see Leo Baeck, *Judaism and Christianity* (Jewish Publication Society, 1958), "Mystery and Commandment."

Chapter 3. Using Reason

For full text, see Moses Maimonides, *The Guide of the Perplexed* (University of Chicago, 1963), translated by Shlomo Pines.

For other discussions on a reasoned faith, see Hugo Bergmann, *Faith and Reason* (B'nai B'rith Hillel Books, 1961); Milton Steinberg, *Anatomy of Faith* (Harcourt Brace, 1960), "The Common Sense of Religious Faith."

Part II. CREATING A GOOD SOCIETY

Chapter 4. Visiting the Sick

For Jewish attitude toward health, see Cohen, *Everyman's Talmud,* Chapter 8; Samuel Cohon, *Judaism, A Way of Life* (Union of American Hebrew Congregations, 1948), Chapter 10; Abba Hillel Silver, *Where Judaism Differed* (Macmillan, 1956), Chapters 11, 14.

For entire text of *Tractate Nedarim,* see Talmud in English translation (Soncino Press, 1952).

Chapter 5. Educating Children

For modern views on Jewish education, see Samuel Belkin, *Essays in Traditional Jewish Thought* (Philosophical Library, 1956), "Parent as Teacher and Teacher as Parent—A Traditional Jewish View"; Buber, *Between Man and Man* (Macmillan, 1965); Heschel, *The Insecurity of Freedom* (Farrar, Straus, 1966), "Jewish Education"; Mordecai M. Kaplan, *Questions Jews Ask* (Reconstructionist Press, 1956), especially pp. 341–361.

For traditional teachings, see Cohen's *Everyman's Talmud,* Section IV; Louis Ginzberg, *Students, Scholars and Saints*

(Meridian Paperback, 1958); Montefiore and Loewe, *A Rabbinic Anthology,* Chapter 24.

For translation of *Kitzur Shulhan Arukh,* see *Code of Jewish Law,* edited by Hyman Goldin (Hebrew Publishing Co., revised ed., 1963).

Chapter 6. Preserving Life

For discussion of Judaism's affirmation of life over death, see Silver, *Where Judaism Differed,* Chapter 15.

For traditional position on *halakhah,* see Cohen, *Everyman's Talmud,* Chapter 4; Montefiore and Loewe, *A Rabbinic Anthology,* Chapter 5.

For translation of *Tractate Yoma,* see Soncino Talmud.

For story dealing with theme of preserving life, see David Frishman, "Three Who Ate," in Azriel Eisenberg, *Modern Jewish Life in Literature* (United Synagogue Commission on Jewish Education, 1948).

Part III. BELONGING TO THE JEWISH PEOPLE

Chapter 7. Loving the Land

For story of rebuilding in pre-State days, see Maurice Samuel, *Harvest in the Desert* (Jewish Publication Society, 1944).

For relationship between Jewish people and Land of Israel, see Buber, *Israel and The World* (Schocken, 2nd ed., 1963), "The Land and Its Possessors" and *Israel and Palestine* (East and West Library, 1952).

For meaning of Zionism before birth of Israel, see Mordecai M. Kaplan, *A New Zionism* (Herzl Press, 1955).

For full text of *The Kuzari,* see translation by Hartwig Hirschfeld (Pardes, 1946; Schocken, 1964).

Chapter 8. Being True to the Jewish People

For another essay on related theme, see "Imitation and Assimilation," in *Selected Essays by Ahad Ha-am,* translated by Leon Simon (World, 1962). See also Arthur Hertzberg, *The Zionist Idea* (Doubleday and Herzl Press, 1959).

For discussion of Jewish self-hatred, see Nathan Glazer, *American Judaism* (University of Chicago, 1957), especially last chapter; Milton Steinberg, *The Making of the Modern Jew* (Behrman House, 1952), Chapters 11 and 12.

Part IV. SERVING GOD

Chapter 9. Prayer

See Solomon Freehof, *The Small Sanctuary* (Union of American Hebrew Congregations, 1942); Robert Gordis, *A Faith for Moderns* (Bloch, 1960); Haim Greenberg, *The Inner Eye* (Jewish Frontier Association, 1964), Vol. II; Heschel, *Man's Quest for God* (Scribner, 1954); *Reconstructionist Sabbath Prayerbook* (Reconstructionist Press, 1953), Introduction.

No full English translation of *Hovot Halevavot* exists as yet.

Chapter 10. Study

For another view of East European Jewish study and scholarship, see Ginzberg, *Students, Scholars and Sages,* especially "The Disciple of the Wise" and "The Rabbinical Student."

For bitter attack on old-style *yeshivah,* based on personal experience, see *The Autobiography of Solomon Maimon* (Schocken, 1947).

For traditional attitudes on study, see George F. Moore, "The

Idea of Torah in Judaism," in *The Menorah Treasury* edited by Leo Schwarz (Jewish Publication Society, 1964).

For modern pleas for Jewish study, see Franz Rosenzweig "On Jewish Learning," in Nahum Glatzer, *Franz Rosenzweig* (Schocken, 1961); and Buber, *Israel and the World,* Sections II and III.

Chapter 11. Observing the Sabbath

For a picture of Sabbath in history, custom, literature and song, see Heschel, *The Sabbath* (Farrar, Straus and Young, 1951); Abraham Millgram, *The Sabbath, Day of Delight* (Jewish Publication Society, 1944); Hayyim Schauss, *The Jewish Festivals* (Union of American Hebrew Congregations, 1938); Solomon Schechter, *Some Aspects of Rabbinic Theology* (Behrman House, 1936), Chapter 8.

No English translation of *Hok Leyisrael* exists as yet.

Chapter 12. Loving God

For modern interpretations, see Buber, *Israel and the World* ("The Love of God and the Idea of Deity"), and *At the Turning* (Farrar, Straus and Young, 1952), final chapter; Heschel, *Man Is Not Alone,* Part I and *God in Search of Man,* Part I (Meridian Paperback, 1961); Kaplan, *The Greater Judaism in the Making* (Reconstructionist Press, 1960), pp. 467–474; "Yossel Rakover's Appeal to God" in Zvi Kolitz, *The Tiger Beneath the Skin* (Creative Age Press, 1947).

For full text of *Mesillat Yesharim,* see translation by Mordecai M. Kaplan (Jewish Publication Society, 1936).

Index